FROM
COMFORT
ZONE TO
TRUST
ZONE

OW JESUS URGES US TO TAKE LEAPS OF FAITH FOR HIS KINGDOM

CECIL TAYLOR

From Comfort Zone to Trust Zone: How Jesus Urges Us to Take Leaps of Faith for His Kingdom

Copyright 2024 by Cecil Taylor

All rights reserved.

Paperback ISBN 978-1-957497-34-1

Printed in the United States of America

Contents

Now Entering the Trust Zone

When we commit to becoming disciples of Christ, we need to understand what it means to be a disciple. What does Jesus require of us? What do those requirements mean to our daily lives? How can we apply the stories and sayings of Jesus to life situations?

As I read the Gospels, I'm struck by how often Jesus challenges people, urging them to leave their pasts behind, to immediately follow him, to repent and change their ways, to take risks, to do uncomfortable things to serve his kingdom, to trust utterly with faith that at its fullest would move mountains.

[1] The very first disciples, as described in the Gospel of John, are thought to be Andrew and John. They learned quickly about Jesus' challenges to take risks. Scripture tells us they quit following John the Baptist to literally follow behind Jesus, who turned and asked them, "What are you looking for?"

They answered, "Rabbi, where are you staying?" Their intent was to have a deeper conversation with Jesus, to build a deeper relationship. And Jesus replied, "Come and see!"

Come and see! Jesus made no promises of what their discipling lives would be like. He didn't offer a salary or benefits or even a job description. He essentially said, "Dive in, and you'll figure it out."

Jesus still instructs us to dive in today. Jesus is looking for new, risk-taking disciples *today* to join him in his kingdom on earth. And he's looking for his current disciples to also take risks and go deeper in their faith and trust.

From Comfort Zone to Trust Zone is a Bible study that explores a dozen ways that Jesus urges you to move from your comfort zone into his trust zone – the place where you come and see, the place where you dive in, where you go deeper with him, where you move mountains with faith, where his kingdom is revealed.

Comfort Zones vs. Trust Zones

"Comfort zone" is a familiar term. I imagine we hear this phrase almost every day.

"Trust zone" is a term I made up – as far as I know. Thus, it needs definition.

What is a comfort zone, and what might a trust zone be? I asked this of a class I was teaching. Some of their brainstorming ideas:

COMFORT ZONE
- Easy
- Safe
- Peaceful
- Familiar
- People you know
- Confident
- Rest

- Relaxed
- Hassle-free
- No risk

TRUST ZONE
- Out of comfort zone
- In danger
- Safety net
- Feeling free to speak
- Comfortably vulnerable
- No judgment
- Trusting

What struck me about their perceptions is that a trust zone may contain risk and danger, but it also includes comfort and safety of its own.

Clearly, I don't expect you to feel comfortable about leaving your comfort zone. My role is to point out what Jesus said and did, and to help push you toward the new, the ambiguous, the uncertain. But you won't be alone there. Because as we'll learn, Jesus is always with you in the trust zone.

A Trust Zone Analogy

I have a hobby of ascending tall towers wherever I travel: The Empire State Building and CN Tower in North America, the Eiffel Tower and Vienna Tower in Europe, Taipei 101 and Tokyo Skytree in Asia, Melbourne Skydeck in Australia, and many more famous and not-so-well-known towers. I love the views where I can learn about the surrounding area. I look forward to the elevator journeys up and down, which with new technology, are becoming faster all the time. I enjoy the stories of how these towers were built.

These days, many of them have added a clear floor, upon which you can stand, look down through your feet, and see the ground hundreds of feet below. The first such floor I visited is previously pictured, at Calgary Tower. Those aren't my feet, but that is indeed the view I saw and remember!

It's a disconcerting experience; all of your senses warn you that you are in danger of falling, yet you're actually standing on a solid, secure platform.

Now Entering the Trust Zone

The most wicked tower glass experience I witnessed was at Melbourne Skydeck. It's a skyscraper with an observation deck and a "torture chamber" you pay for called Edge. Adventurous visitors enter an enclosed glass cube that slides out horizontally from the building, seemingly without any support. I wasn't so adventurous, so I decided to watch from a side point of view to see its operation before I tried it.

I don't know if Skydeck does this anymore, but when I visited in 2010, the cube's glass was tinted so you couldn't see out as the cube slid into the sky. Here's the wicked part: The cube would stop, and the tinted color would seem to fall, replaced by transparency, at the same moment that the sound of shattering glass was played! The effect was to momentarily make you think that the cube had been shattered, and you were going to fall.

It's a scream-o ride. People experienced a terrifying instant, then laughter would follow. For some. The rest were still shaken. I watched this several times and decided Edge wasn't for me.

Grand Canyon Skywalk is a 10-foot wide, horseshoe-shaped glass bridge that extends 70 feet out over the canyon. While I'm fascinated by glass floors, my senses twang too much for me to walk such a distance without freaking out!

I took this selfie while lying on the transparent floor at Lotte Tower in Seoul, clowning around, knowing it was safe. Yet I could not bring myself to put my whole body on the clear surface, although that floor is probably as sturdy and supportive as the surrounding concrete. But I was lying on a trust zone, right?

This is what it's like when we obey Jesus' urging to take risks for His kingdom. We're actually led to solid ground, perhaps the most solid ground we've ever stood upon, but it doesn't look like it. It's like a glass floor. It feels uncomfortable, disorienting, and even hazardous. We worry that the structure will collapse, and we may fall at any moment. But Jesus will support us when we take those risks, loving us, providing help, even carrying us if we need it. That's when you're in Jesus' trust zone.

Challenging Your Faith

I found this quote to be most interesting and worth considering. It comes from Alexander Lang, a former pastor who became burned out in his job. Here's one reason.

> Most Christians don't want their thinking challenged. They come to church to reinforce what they've believed their entire lives. From their perspective, the job of the pastor is not to push them to grow, but to reassure them that they are already on the right track. Any learning should support the party line and comfort them that their investment of resources in the church will result in a payoff somewhere down the line, particularly once they reach the afterlife. [2]

This book may indeed show you that you are on the right track, in some ways. But this book will also challenge your faith and push you to grow.

There are 12 comfort zones and 12 corresponding trust zones identified in this book.

- You may find that some comfort zones do not apply to you. You are past those comfort zones and are already in the corresponding trust zones.

- You may find that a comfort zone sort of applies to you. You can see where you can improve your faith walk by following the description of the trust zone.
- You may find comfort zone descriptions that hit a nerve, that make your cheeks turn red with shame or make your blood boil with anger. Pay close attention to these, because you have located your cherished comfort zones, and you should seriously consider how to leap from them to the corresponding trust zones. This is where you can grow your faith. But you're going to have to change, leaving behind something you have long believed or followed. Listen closely to what Jesus has to say to you through scripture and through this book.

Now let's start our study of 12 Bible stories in which Jesus challenges people to enter a trust zone, learning how to apply these stories to our 7-day practical faith journey.

Taking Risks

Bravado. Courageous. Boldness. Audacity. Adventuresome.

You might find these words in a thesaurus to represent risk-taking and risk-takers. They certainly sound accurate on the surface.

Then again, I know this phrase as well: "Sometimes not taking a risk is taking a risk." Life calls us forward whether we want to take a risk or not. It can be dicey to try to stay in the same comfortable place.

What I want to show in this chapter is that there is another side of risk-taking that should inform us Christians as we strive to live a 7-day practical faith. It is a dimension of attitude, priority, and obligation, all in the service of God.

I would never skydive. Uh-uh. Too risky! But I would (and did) quit my job to fully launch Cecil Taylor Ministries, because I sensed over a period of years that I was called to do so.

If God ever called me to skydive, I would have to reconsider. Thankfully, that call will probably never come!

A Parable of Risk-Taking

The core Bible passage for this chapter is also the core passage for the entire book. It has traditionally been labeled as the Parable of the Talents, but I opt for an updated label called the Parable of the Bags of Gold.

The reason is that the word "talent" gives us English speakers the wrong impression. We think of talents as gifts or abilities. But back in Biblical days, "talents" indicated weight. When the parable reads that a person was given five talents, that indicates the measure of the weight of the coins or gold handed over.

With that in mind, let's examine the Parable of the Bags of Gold, as Jesus tells the tale in Matthew 25: 14-30.

"Again, it will be like a man going on a journey, who called his servants and entrusted his wealth to them. To one he gave five bags of gold, to another two bags, and to another one bag, each according to his ability. Then he went on his journey. The man who had received five bags of gold went at once and put his money to work and gained five bags more. So also, the one with two bags of gold gained two more. But the man who had received one bag went off, dug a hole in the ground and hid his master's money.

[3] "After a long time the master of those servants returned and settled accounts with them. The man who had received five bags of gold brought the other five. 'Master,' he said, 'you entrusted me with five bags of gold. See, I have gained five more.'

"His master replied, 'Well done, good and faithful servant! You have been faithful with a few things; I will put you in charge of many things. Come and share your master's happiness!'

"The man with two bags of gold also came. 'Master,' he said, 'you entrusted me with two bags of gold; see, I have gained two more.'

"His master replied, 'Well done, good and faithful servant! You have been faithful with a few things; I will put you in charge of many things. Come and share your master's happiness!'

"Then the man who had received one bag of gold came. 'Master,' he said, 'I knew that you are a hard man, harvesting where you have not sown and gathering where you have not scattered seed. So I was afraid and went out and hid your gold in the ground. See, here is what belongs to you.'

"His master replied, 'You wicked, lazy servant! So you knew that I harvest where I have not sown and gather where I have not scattered seed? Well then, you should have put my money on deposit with the bankers, so that when I returned I would have received it back with interest.

"'So take the bag of gold from him and give it to the one who has ten bags. For whoever has will be given more, and they will have an abundance. Whoever does not have, even what they have will be taken from them. And throw that worthless servant outside, into the darkness, where there will be weeping and gnashing of teeth.'

Scottish theologian William Barclay wrote, "In this parable Jesus tells us that there can be no religion without adventure." [4] To what adventure is Christ calling you?

Let's clarify a few things about the parable. The bags of gold belong to the master (meaning, God). They never belong to the individual. Any benefits from managing the money also go to the master. It's not clear what percentage, if any, goes to the servant.

The master is pleased with those who invested and doubled his money. To invest means to take a risk. If you've ever invested, you know that there are few promises about the return. Financial caveats state that the more return you seek, the bigger the associated risk. The two servants who were able to double the master's money took big, risky swings to do so.

The servants were given bags of gold to work with. What do

these bags of gold represent? Ray Stedman points out that they stand for opportunities:

> (The bags of gold) represent the opportunities that come to us, as professing Christians, to invest and utilize the natural abilities that God has given us, not on our behalf, but for Christ's sake...
>
> They are moments of fateful decision when we are confronted with the question of whether we are willing to invest our life and risk the loss of something we want, in order that God may have something he wants...
>
> These opportunities to invest your life for his sake or save it for yourself are God-given opportunities which he provides. In that fateful moment we hang between heaven and hell, a moment of crisis and decision.[5]

The first two servants took that risk for the sake of their master. But the third servant did not.

That servant hid the money and returned to the master the same sum given. The master was furious because the servant did not at least invest the money in a bank for some nominal, low-risk return.

Here's a question: Exactly what did the third servant do while the master was gone? He clearly wasn't acting in the master's interests. It's easy to conclude that the servant was lazy, but I think the problem goes deeper than that.

My conclusion is that the third servant was working for *himself*.

Just as he did not invest the money, he also invested neither time nor energy on the master's behalf. The servant felt no debt or obligation to the master. He selfishly worked for himself, ignoring the opportunities the master gave him, and then came up with a lame, rather rude excuse when called to account. Stedman interprets the third servant's excuse in this way:

> (The servant) says to (the master), in effect, "Look. When it all boils down to final things, it's your fault. I knew you, knew the kind of man you are. You're a hard, grasping individual. You expect people to do your dirty work for you, but you get all the benefits. You are unreasonable in your demands. If people don't come through with what you expect, you blame them for it. But I've outwitted you. I've got exactly what you gave me. Here it is. You and I are even."[6]

The master saw this wicked servant as wasting a huge opportunity and punished him for his lack of consideration and service.

The Parable's Comfort and Trust Zones

In this parable, the comfort zone is our desire for comfort and security and doing things our way. We want to play it safe. We want to "do our thing." We don't want to leave our comfort zone to do something extra for God.

The trust zone is the place where we seize opportunities for the master's behalf. We're given the freedom and command to leverage those opportunities, but always with kingdom goals in mind, not ours.

In summary, the conflict between the comfort zones and trust zones in this parable boils down to whom we are working for. Our comfort zone is self-interest and self-preservation. Our trust zone is self-denial on behalf of the Lord.

Let me pose this question. What do you think would have happened if one of the servants had invested and taken a risk, but it did not return enough money?

This is a good discussion question with valid points on each side. (If you are in a group study, this is one of the questions offered for discussion in the Leader Guide).

My view is that the master would still have been pleased, as the servant did the right thing in entering the trust zone and taking a risk. We are first called to be faithful before we're called to be successful.

It also depends on your view of success. In God's calculation, something that looks unsuccessful to humans may be very successful. Our actions have a ripple effect; perhaps someone was influenced to learn from our efforts or was encouraged to take a risk themselves. God repurposes failure and calamity for good.

Of course, we all want to hear, "Well done, good and faithful servant! Come and share your master's happiness!" We want to hear it in prayer or in spirit here on earth; we want to hear it when we come face to face with Jesus. God's opportunities can only be leveraged when we take a risk.

The Elephant in the Room

In practically every book and video series I produce, there is a section called "The Elephant in the Room." I realize there is always a counter argument to the key points I present, and I want to address that elephant up front.

In this case, you might wonder, "Doesn't Jesus want us to be comfortable? Is he always calling us to go forward? Is everything in our lives supposed to be about risk?"

My response, quoting Ecclesiastes 3:1, is, "There is a time for everything." Indeed, there are times when the Holy Spirit will tell you "no," instead of "yes." Times when the Spirit says, "Clear your calendar" or "it's time to focus on your family." We can experience fallow times of rest or repair or waiting. We sometimes require dormancy, replenishment, nourishment, and pruning. It's not always go-go-go.

But realize that the slower periods often set up the action. In the long run, Jesus urges us to keep going forward and to take leaps of faith for His kingdom.

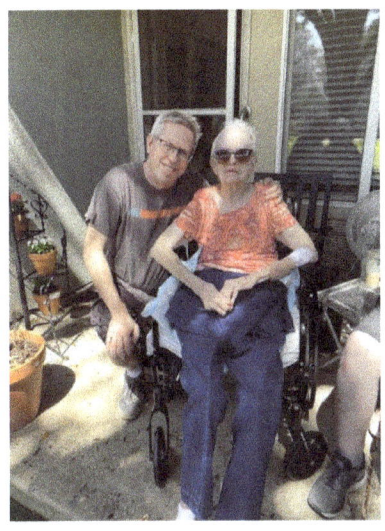

Let me give you an example of how the Spirit's leadership can alternate between go and don't-go. As soon as I took a leap of faith, quitting my day job in 2021 to turn Cecil Taylor Ministries into a full-time venture, my mother's health took a drastic turn for the worse.

She lived near me, and I was her primary caregiver. Instead of working full-time on the ministry, I was spending significant time on her care.

I kept praying on this matter, asking God, "Why did you bring me to this point when I was supposed to start a ministry, and instead, I'm a caregiver?" I mean, clearly, it was good that without fulltime employment, I had time flexibility to help her, but still! God's consistent response was, "You're the only one who can do what you're doing. Take care of your mother. I'm patient. When the time comes, we'll work together on the ministry."

In other words, stop and wait. Your new ministry trust zone can be delayed.

Of course, you may observe that the caregiving itself wasn't truly a restful time, but was itself a trust zone, where I needed to lean on Jesus to sustain me through the effort. And of course, you can correctly guess that God has used every ounce of that experience to inform my ministry as I have moved forward into a new trust zone.

A Connection to the Parable

Even in those fallow times, we're not usually called to be completely inactive. Even in those times, there are times of service and self-denial.

To put it in the context of the Parable of the Bags of Gold, our abilities may be compromised at times. Not necessarily our skills, talents, and gifts, but our *ability to respond.* For example, when I was helping my mother, my ability to respond to my perceived call, and other volunteer needs, was reduced.

How can we still enter trust zones when we're at a disadvantage in our ability to respond, for whatever reason?

I'm reminded of this story that emerged from a youth mission trip on which I was a sponsor.

Our youth group and adult leaders had traveled to Galveston months after Hurricane Ike to help remodel homes damaged by the storm. I was leading a group of seniors, so we were assigned one of the toughest jobs, remodeling a small "shotgun house" in an

impoverished neighborhood near the Port of Galveston.

A challenge came to us almost immediately. The residents were not there, as the house was unlivable, so the electricity had been turned off. We needed to use circular saws and other equipment to do the work. What could we do?

Taking Risks

We talked with the neighbor next door; his house had also been damaged, but he was able to live in it while his name sat on a wait list for volunteer attention. He agreed to let us run electrical cords to his house to draw power for our work, although his home's electrical capability was such that it would give out several times during the day.

But this neighbor did more than offer electricity. He provided bottles of water and a few snacks. Since it was brutally hot and humid working in a house with no air conditioning, the man offered his living room as a break room for our team during our week in Galveston.

Even though his abilities were diminished in his situation, the neighbor still served God's work as he could. He entered a trust zone to allow smelly strangers to spend time in his living room.

The neighbor could be exempted from criticism as someone with his own waitlisted needs. But instead, he took a risk and helped us help his absent neighbor.

The bottom line is, the Holy Spirit will sometimes tap the brakes, but we must always be aware of our obligation to serve God's kingdom and to do whatever we can.

Summary of "Taking Risks"

Big Thought:
God rewards us when we take risks on the Kingdom's behalf.

Core Passage:
Matthew 25: 14-30

Key verse: 'Well done, good and faithful servant! You have been faithful with a few things; I will put you in charge of many things. Come and share your master's happiness!'

The Comfort Zone:
Self-interest and self-preservation.

The Trust Zone:
Self-denial to serve the Lord's interests.

Going All-In

The sixth chapter of John describes a wild time in Jesus' ministry, where his popularity rose and fell within a single chapter.

[7] It starts with thousands of people showing up to hear Jesus preach. He winds up feeding them all through a miracle of transforming five barley loaves and two small fish. Many people follow him as a result, adding to the growing throng.

But by the end of the chapter, Jesus is saying strange things, to their ears. He claims to have come down from heaven, that he is God's son, and he has actually seen God. He promises never-ending life for those who believe in what he's saying, but they must eat his flesh and drink his blood.

Now the people are wondering, "Who is this guy? Is he a rebel? Is he a crackpot? Is he proposing cannibalism?" And this is where we join the text, in verse 60, ending with verse 69.

On hearing it, many of his disciples said, "This is a hard teaching. Who can accept it?"

Aware that his disciples were grumbling about this, Jesus said to them, "Does this offend you? Then what if you see the

Son of Man ascend to where he was before! The Spirit gives life; the flesh counts for nothing. The words I have spoken to you—they are full of the Spirit and life. Yet there are some of you who do not believe." For Jesus had known from the beginning which of them did not believe and who would betray him. He went on to say, "This is why I told you that no one can come to me unless the Father has enabled them."

From this time many of his disciples turned back and no longer followed him.

"You do not want to leave too, do you?" Jesus asked the Twelve.

Simon Peter answered him, "Lord, to whom shall we go? You have the words of eternal life. We have come to believe and to know that you are the Holy One of God."

This passage shows the drastic impact of Jesus' teaching on the crowd: most walk away. When confronted with spiritual needs and a spiritual message, most people turn it down. The more Jesus insists on being the means to eternal life, the angrier the crowd becomes, until the vast majority simply abandon Him. [8]

Jesus urged this mass of followers to leave their comfort zones. What comfort zones were they in, and why did they not want to go all-in on Jesus, like his core group of disciples?

The Opt-Out Disciples

I see three reasons why these disciples decided to opt out at this point in Jesus' ministry.

Some followers loved taking from Jesus when he was doling out food and healing, but now he was asking them to buy in and to give of themselves. The truth is, even today, there are people who want to take from Jesus but not give back. They're in a comfort zone where church is for their entertainment, where tithing is to be overlooked, and where giving back is not their intent. But Jesus calls for us to give back.

The question is, are you giving back to Jesus and to the people he loves?

The second group of followers in this story was concerned that Jesus and his band of disciples were on a collision course with the authorities. You couldn't say things like Jesus was saying and get away with it. It wasn't the norm. The truth is, even today, there are people who want to align with culture and society and don't want to rock the boat. They don't want to be weird or an outcast or looked down upon. But Jesus promised us that if we truly follow him, we'll be maligned in one way or another.

The question is, are you maligned enough, persecuted enough, to suit Jesus?

The third reason to depart is that some followers just were not ready and willing to go all-in with Jesus. They weren't sure what that would look like and what would be required of them. They wanted some of what Jesus was offering but wanted to protect their hearts for themselves, for their own plans, for their own desires. The truth is, we can do the same, accepting Jesus, but only on our own terms.

The question is, are you negotiating with Jesus to only do what meets your needs and makes you feel comfortable?

I Thought I Was All-In, But…

I can identify these reasons in the deserters because they are part of my story as well, especially the last two reasons.

As I mentioned in the prior chapter, in 2009, I joined a mission trip with the youth of my church, visiting Galveston, Texas, which had been wracked by Hurricane Ike. During the day, we worked extremely hard to repair homes damaged by the flooding. During the evening, we worshipped. In one of those worship times, we held a long prayer session.

I was already involved in so many things at my church: Teaching Adult Sunday School, teaching parenting classes, meeting with the youth on Sunday nights – actually, at that time, our church was short-staffed, and I was leading the middle school program. I also met with a male student small group, doing life together. And I was thinking about taking on a second group of high school seniors that were in my mission trip small group and really needed some work, in my view. I was serving, serving, serving.

So in the prayer session, I promised God that if desired, I would lead that second group, and I asked for guidance. But then I heard the Spirit's voice, clear as a bell, saying, "I don't want you to lead another group. What I want is your heart!"

I immediately burst into tears because I was busted.

I thought I had somehow hidden from God that I was giving back with my body and my time, but not with my heart. I thought serving by doing what was comfortable to me was enough, but...

I wasn't all-in. I was holding back parts of myself because I didn't want to rock the boat and possibly be weird for Jesus. I didn't want to give over full control of my life, because I didn't know what he would ask me to do if I did. It would be fair to say that I exhibited, to some degree, all three issues of these hesitant followers in John 6.

That night in Galveston, I decided to go all-in and give my heart fully to God. I didn't know exactly what that meant; what I learned is probably another entire book on its own! But my life has been different ever since.

Jesus Requires Full Participation

The phrase "all-in" comes from gambling, where someone bets all their chips, or money on the table, on a single wager. You make a mint, or you leave empty-handed.

Jesus wants people to go all-in on him, on what he's saying, on what he requires. A passage from Luke 9: 57-62 comes to mind, as Jesus encountered three men who said they wanted to be his disciple.

> As they were walking along the road, a man said to him, "I will follow you wherever you go." Jesus replied, "Foxes have dens and birds have nests, but the Son of Man has no place to lay his head."
>
> He said to another man, "Follow me." But he replied, "Lord, first let me go and bury my father." Jesus said to him, "Let the dead bury their own dead, but you go and proclaim the kingdom of God."
>
> Still another said, "I will follow you, Lord; but first let me go back and say goodbye to my family." Jesus replied,

"No one who puts a hand to the plow and looks back is fit for service in the kingdom of God."

Jesus' response to the first man's promise is to check the cost of his willingness. He didn't want the man to misunderstand what was required of his disciples. Sacrifice and discomfort, to name a couple of things.

The second man wanted to wait until his father had died before joining Jesus. Christ's response seems harsh: "Let the dead bury the dead." But if the man's father had already died, he would be involved in the funeral. Instead, the father was still alive, the burial was not imminent, and in fact, it might be years away. The man was wanting to delay until his father had finally passed away before becoming a disciple. But Christ wasn't having any of it, telling him in essence, "You need to follow me now and put me off no longer."

Jesus labels the third man as unfit for waffling at the moment of decision. Imagine if the man went to say goodbye to his loved ones; they might talk him out of following Jesus. Christ desires our full commitment, with no regrets, no looking back. Other disciples had followed his command to drop what they were doing and follow him. This man needed to do the same.

In each case, Jesus was telling the men – and us – to go all-in. We can't start following him and wonder if we are truly committed to the cost of discipleship. We can't stall our participation in his kingdom until a more convenient time. We can't look back once we join him. Christ insists on our wholehearted pledge to leave our comfort zones and enter the trust zone to become his disciple and to follow through on what God wants of us.

Opt-Out / All-In Comfort and Trust Zones

In the stories within this chapter, we see a number of comfort zones specific to the individual. But they all relate to the same question: Who's in charge here?

Going All-In

The common comfort zone is that these people all wanted Jesus on their terms, for their convenience, as they could fit him into their schedule, if he wasn't too demanding or challenging or weird, if he didn't ask too much of them.

Even though we think about God as being interested in the long run of eternity, the truth of the Gospel is that there is an immediacy, an urgency, to everything that Jesus does. It's not that he is impatient, as the Fruit of the Spirit includes patience, and Jesus exhibits all fruits perfectly. Lord knows he is patiently waiting for each one of us to fully accept his invitation! But there's no question that the Jesus of the Gospels isn't concerned if his message offends us or challenges us. He wants us to join him in the present. Jesus considers the present a time zone where the moment and the eternal can intertwine. [i]

The trust zone, then, is accepting Jesus on his terms, in his time, ready to drop what we're doing, plowing forward, eager to do his will and to see what he has in store for us next. Going all-in.

Norman Vincent Peale compared our faith walk to a track and field high jump, saying, "Throw your heart over the bar, and your body will follow." [9] Let's lead with our hearts, giving them fully to Christ, and follow where he will take us.

---

[i]   For an expansion on this thought, please see the "Live Like You're Eternal" chapters of my book, "Live Like You're Loved."

Summary of "Going All-In"

Big Thought:
Jesus wants us to fully participate in his kingdom as soon as possible, holding nothing back.

Core Passage:
John 6: 60-69

Key verse: "The words I have spoken to you—they are full of the Spirit and life. Yet there are some of you who do not believe."

The Comfort Zone:
Accepting Jesus on our terms.

The Trust Zone:
Following Jesus on his terms.

Replacing Status-Seeking with Servanthood

The end of his ministry was coming. Jesus knew it as he prepared for the Last Supper with his disciples, the cross already casting a shadow over his final hours.

But his disciples weren't as concerned about the future as where everyone would sit at the Last Supper table. So Jesus had one final lesson to teach them.

I want to glue together two stories from the Last Supper accounts of Luke and John to paint a more complete picture of one of the seminal moments in Jesus' instruction of his disciples, when he humbly washed their feet.

Before I dive in, I want to state something that I normally say when teaching the Bible. To me, in the Old Testament, the Hebrews represent us modern-day disciples. They became disobedient and then repented in a never-ending cycle. In the New Testament, Jesus' 12 disciples represent us. We laugh at the disciples for not getting what Jesus was saying. But so many times, neither do we.

Thus, as we read the accounts of misbehaving, clueless, ornery disciples in this chapter, we must humbly put ourselves in their position and realize that their foibles are also ours.

The Status-Seeking of the Disciples

Jesus' heart must have been heavy as he and the disciples gathered in the upper room for their final meal together. Then the disciples started jockeying for position. Imagine preparing to visit your mother dying in the hospital while your kids argue over seating positions in the car.

Here is the story from Luke 22: 24-27.

A dispute also arose among them as to which of them was considered to be greatest. Jesus said to them, "The kings of the Gentiles lord it over them; and those who exercise authority over them call themselves Benefactors. But you are not to be like that. Instead, the greatest among you should be like the youngest, and the one who rules like the one who serves. For who is greater, the one who is at the table or the one who serves? Is it not the one who is at the table? But I am among you as one who serves.

[10] Why would the disciples argue over which was the greatest? Because of seating arrangements. At a Jewish feast, the guest of highest honor sat to the right of the host; on the host's left was the second-ranked guest. The third guest sat second to the right; the

fourth guest sat second to the left, and so forth. What we just read was a scriptural seating squabble.

Jesus used this petty moment to point out his priorities for true honor, based on servanthood and meekness.

Status-Seeking Today

Let's map this into our behaviors today. What are the ways that we seek status?

- Wanting that promotion and the corner office.
  - o Not even the corner office – wanting the best cubicle to reflect our organizational position.
- Joining a gang to be cool and identified in a certain way.
- Focusing on how many followers we have and how many likes we receive.
- Aspiring to achieve fame as a TikTok influencer.
- Trying risky adventures in order to gain attention.
- Hoping our child will be the first in the extended family to get married or have a baby. "I could be the first grandparent of my generation!"
- Focusing on how our wedding will look on Instagram rather than the relationship with others in the wedding party or even what the marriage will become.
- Identifying ourselves through the clothing and accessories we wear.
- Name-dropping to make ourselves look more important.
- Using products and services to represent our desired position.
  - o Buying or renting expensive items to signal our wealth.
  - o Flaunting the ways we are more environmentally friendly or socially responsible than others.

Note that the motivation, not the action, is what defines status-seeking. Aspiring to be a grandparent or to help the world overcome climate change are good desires, but the motivations may not be pure.

The Last Supper from Another Angle

John tells a different story at the Last Supper that likely referred to the same event. The timing of the stories is different, and other details are different, but both stories land in the same space, with Jesus stressing the importance of humility and servanthood.

Again, to set the scene: This is the last time that Jesus will be with the disciples, his last chance to pour into them. He has a lot to say: John 13 through 17, five chapters, are pretty much all red in a red-letter Bible that highlights Jesus' words. But what is the starting point? What is the first, possibly most important lesson he wants to share? Let's start at the beginning of John 13 (verses 1-5, then 12-17).

It was just before the Passover Festival. Jesus knew that the hour had come for him to leave this world and go to the Father. Having loved his own who were in the world, he loved them to the end.

The evening meal was in progress, and the devil had already prompted Judas, the son of Simon Iscariot, to betray Jesus. Jesus knew that the Father had put all things under his power, and that he had come from God and was returning to God; so he got up from the meal, took off his outer clothing, and wrapped a towel around his waist. After that, he poured water into a basin and began to wash his disciples' feet, drying them with the towel that was wrapped around him.

[11] When he had finished washing their feet, he put on his clothes and returned to his place. "Do you understand what I have done for you?" he asked them. "You call me 'Teacher' and 'Lord,' and rightly so, for that is what I am. Now that I, your Lord and Teacher, have washed your feet, you also should wash one another's feet. I have set you an example that you should do as I have done for you. Very truly I tell you, no servant is greater than his master, nor is a messenger greater than the one who sent him. Now that you know these things, you will be blessed if you do them.

Washing the smelly feet of dirt-road travelers was a job for a lowly servant. If no servant was available, then one of the traveling party might wash the feet of the others. It's possible that this was part of the disciples' dispute; their concerns weren't just about table seating and being the greatest, but also about service and being the lowliest.

Jesus himself did what none of them was prepared to do. [12] It was one of the final teaching moments from Jesus to the disciples to illustrate how they should emulate his humble leadership.

The comfort zone is not simply about seeking status. It's also about our unwillingness to stoop low and get our hands dirty. But because Jesus did it, we should follow.

One of my constant themes in teaching Christians to live a 7-day practical faith is that we need to get better, individually and collectively, about actually doing what Jesus told us to do. Here is a convicting example of our failures.

Gandhi's Critique

There is a famous quote attributed to Mahatma Gandhi: "I like your Christ. I do not like your Christians. Your Christians are so unlike your Christ."

While it's hard to find the source of that exact quote, it's easier to find several similar variations that Gandhi did say. For example, in The Christ of the Indian Road, E. Stanley Jones quotes Gandhi saying during an interview about Christian evangelism in India, "I would suggest first of all that all of you Christians, missionaries and all begin to live more like Jesus Christ." [13]

Regardless of exact wording, to hear someone outside of Christianity say that we Christians do not emulate Jesus is a bitter pill to swallow. Some will take it as conviction. Others will lash back at the source.

One of the latter was a Christian author who railed at length in his blog about Gandhi creating a Jesus of his own making, without understanding the fullness of Christ and how he is the one who was and is and is to come. The author accused Gandhi of reflecting his own values upon Jesus and loving that version of Jesus. He even compared Gandhi to Pharisees who surely did not love the outspoken Jesus they encountered.

I read this author's rant a couple of times and noticed a serious omission:

Nowhere did the author defend Christian behavior.

Nowhere did he say that Gandhi was wrong about how well or poorly Christians emulate Jesus.

For my part, I take Gandhi's comments to heart. He is obviously not alone in surveying Christian behavior and deciding that it falls well short of Jesus' standards.

Certainly, we followers can point out that we ourselves are not Christ and that we will always disappoint anyone holding us to perfection. I have no quarrel with that argument. But Jesus still gave us a lot of instruction with which we fail to comply. One of those instructions is how to adopt an attitude of meekness and serve others. Jesus indeed was and is and is to come, but he can handle that part himself, without our help. Our assignment is to wash the feet of others.

Parallel Passages

Jesus' instruction at the Last Supper wasn't the first time the disciples had heard that theme. Here are a few examples from the Gospels.

Matthew 18: 1-4 reads:

> At that time the disciples came to Jesus and asked, "Who, then, is the greatest in the kingdom of heaven?"
>
> He called a little child to him and placed the child among them. And he said: "Truly I tell you, unless you change and become like little children, you will never enter the kingdom of heaven. Therefore, whoever takes the lowly position of this child is the greatest in the kingdom of heaven."

Luke 14: 7-11:

> When he noticed how the guests picked the places of honor at the table, he told them this parable:

"When someone invites you to a wedding feast, do not take the place of honor, for a person more distinguished than you may have been invited. If so, the host who invited both of you will come and say to you, 'Give this person your seat.' Then, humiliated, you will have to take the least important place. But when you are invited, take the lowest place, so that when your host comes, he will say to you, 'Friend, move up to a better place.' Then you will be honored in the presence of all the other guests. For all those who exalt themselves will be humbled, and those who humble themselves will be exalted."

Note in the following passage, Matthew 6: 1-4, that Jesus doesn't say that it's wrong to do righteous things to glorify God, but it's wrong if your aim is to glorify yourself.

"Be careful not to practice your righteousness in front of others to be seen by them. If you do, you will have no reward from your Father in heaven. So when you give to the needy, do not announce it with trumpets, as the hypocrites do in the synagogues and on the streets, to be honored by others. Truly I tell you, they have received their reward in full. But when you give to the needy, do not let your left hand know what your right hand is doing, so that your giving may be in secret. Then your Father, who sees what is done in secret, will reward you."

Jesus calls us to trust his counterculture instructions to seek the lowest place, not the highest place, while we put others above us and serve them. Now, I would warn that there are instances where it could be dangerous to lose identity or power (indeed, in an abusive situation, it may be better to protect ourselves than to get run over). But generally speaking, it should become part of our disciple identity to serve, serve, and serve.

Humble Servanthood in Action

Talk about not letting your left hand know what your right hand is doing. I came across a meaningful example of this concept of humble servanthood in action. In the small town of Geraldine, Alabama, lived a retired farmer named Hody Childress. In 2012, Hody walked into the local pharmacy and approached manager Brooke Walker. "Is there ever anyone that can't pay their bill?"

Of course, the answer was "Yes." So Hody handed her a $100 bill, saying, "This is for anyone who can't afford their prescription. Do not tell a soul that the money came from me. Tell them it's a blessing from God."

A month later, Hody returned with the same question, the same intent, and another $100. And on this went, every month. Brooke began taking money from a secret envelope of Hody's money to help others as needed.

One recipient was Bree Slawgan, whose son Eli was stung by a hornet. She couldn't afford the $800 bill, but the bill disappeared with the comment, "It's been taken care of." [14]

Over the course of a decade, Hody's donations came to more than $10,000. And no one knew where the money came from, except Brooke and himself.

As Hody grew weaker from COPD and other ailments, he knew he would have to share his story if he wanted to continue his donations after he was gone. So Hody told his daughter, Tania Nix, to keep the donations going. Tania said, "I was shocked — I had no idea that he was helping people at the drug store." [15]

Hody passed away on Jan. 1, 2023. Since then, the word has spread. Hody's family and others in the town now donate. Someone called the pharmacy from Washington and offered to pay $100 per month, just like Hody. A Miami resident promised to start a similar fund in their community.

From Comfort Zone to Trust Zone

This is the power of the trust zone of humble servanthood that doesn't seek social status. Good was done before the word got out. When the goodness couldn't be kept secret anymore, it burst out and spread. That is Jesus' plan.

Summary of "Replacing Status-Seeking with Servanthood"

Big Thought:
Jesus eradicates any thought that we should pump up our value through status-seeking. Instead, we are to do the opposite, taking the lowest place to serve others.

Core Passages:
Luke 22: 24-27

Key verse in Luke: "I am among you as one who serves."

John 13: 1-5, 12-17

Key verse in John: "I have set you an example that you should do as I have done for you. Very truly I tell you, no servant is greater than his master, nor is a messenger greater than the one who sent him. Now that you know these things, you will be blessed if you do them."

The Comfort Zone:
Chasing and using worldly acclaim to feel better about ourselves.

The Trust Zone:
Humbly serving others so that others will feel better about Jesus.

Releasing Your Sins and Your Stones

I will start this chapter with a confession: I'm very comfortable with my particular varieties of sin. Too comfortable.

This causes me to do two things:

1. Go easy on myself for my sin.
2. Go harder on others for their sin.

I can look at someone else's sin and condemn it. But if I commit the same act, in my mind, there is justification for doing it. Or it's not really that bad. I went about it differently than that other person, so that makes it all right.

Or, I set up in my mind a ranking of sins. Your sins, by the way, are way up the ladder from mine. They are major sins. Mine are minor sins.

Now, of course, this is not the right approach. I can't tell you how many times the Holy Spirit has convicted me regarding this attitude, usually when I'm thinking about how rotten the other person is; then I'm reminded of my own rottenness.

Sometimes it works; I drop my judgmental attitude immediately. Other times, I argue about the difference in my sins. I do not win that argument.

In this chapter, we'll read about some people who were also too comfortable with their sin. Keep in mind that while these people may look different on the surface, they are not so different underneath. More like two sides of the same coin.

The Pharisees and the Adulteress

On the surface, in this story from John 8: 2-11, the Pharisees are carrying stones (figuratively, anyway), and the adulterous woman is carrying sins. We'll see how they're not so different as they approach Jesus.

[16] At dawn he appeared again in the temple courts, where all the people gathered around him, and he sat down to teach them. The teachers of the law and the Pharisees brought in a woman caught in adultery. They made her stand before the group and said to Jesus, "Teacher, this woman was caught in the act of adultery. In the Law Moses commanded us to stone such women. Now what do you say?" They were using this question as a trap, in order to have a basis for accusing him.

But Jesus bent down and started to write on the ground with his finger. When they kept on questioning him, he straightened up and said to them, "Let any one of you who is without sin be the first to throw a stone at her." Again he stooped down and wrote on the ground.

At this, those who heard began to go away one at a time, the older ones first, until only Jesus was left, with the woman still standing there. Jesus straightened up and asked her, "Woman, where are they? Has no one condemned you?"

"No one, sir," she said.

"Then neither do I condemn you," Jesus declared. "Go now and leave your life of sin."

The Brazen Woman

Let's start on the side of the accused. The woman who was accused of adultery would likely have been either very unlucky or very obvious about what she was doing. To make the accusation that the Pharisees charged, she would have been caught in the act of adultery, and witnesses would be able to testify to what they saw. (Yes, there was a man involved who would have also been subject to the death penalty, but the Pharisees apparently let him go scot-free. I won't further address that imbalance of justice here).

I'm going to assume that the woman was comfortable in what she was doing. In her society, surely, she knew the rules and the risks. Was this the first time she had committed the act with this man (or with others)? Did she become emboldened to the point of carelessness and hence was caught?

Without knowing those answers, unless she was a victim (which is possible), she probably had a good idea that she was breaking Mosaic law and was comfortable with the amorous plan.

Jesus' response to her is mercy – for now. He neither condemns nor endorses her behavior. He simply gives her a second chance.

It may seem that Jesus is letting her off easy. But he instructs her to "go and sin no more." He doesn't say what she did was OK. He doesn't look the other way. Judgment may come in the future, but it doesn't come today. Mercy and a second chance are gifted instead.

Jesus' response shouldn't surprise us. Earlier in the Gospel of John is the famous verse of John 3: 16. But we tend to forget the verse after it, John 3:17. Here they are together, with the notation of where the 17th verse begins.

For God so loved the world that he gave his one and only Son, that whoever believes in him shall not perish but have eternal life. 17 For God did not send his Son into the world to condemn the world, but to save the world through him.

Jesus didn't arrive on earth to condemn; he was born to save. So his mercy is designed to save the woman from sin. Condemnation? Jesus reserves the right to judge those who are not believers, which are the ones who shall not perish but have eternal life. Jesus is patient and gives her the chance to avoid judgment by living a sinless life or by becoming a believer.

I've often wondered what happens next in the story. How does the woman respond?

- "Whew! I'm glad that guy came along! I'm off the hook. I'll have to be more careful next time."
- "Wow, only one man was willing to rescue me. And he told me not to do this again. I had better listen to him. Who was he, anyway? I want to know more about this person who has such wise authority."

No doubt, the woman committed **some** kind of sin going forward; we all do. But did she learn repentance? Did she become less comfortable with sin? Did she trust that this man Jesus was right, and she should follow his direction?

The Judgy Pharisees

On the other side stand the Pharisees, bent on tricking Jesus into either breaking Roman law by authorizing a stoning, or being perceived as breaking Judaic law by letting the woman go free.

Jesus counters their intent with a masterful stroke: Calling out their own sin.

We don't know what Jesus was writing in the dirt; one theory is that he began listing the sins of the people who wanted to stone the woman. Even if he didn't, with his directive that the one without sin could cast the first stone, Jesus caused the Pharisees to mentally list their own sins, release their stones, and walk away.

The episode reminds me of the Parable of the Unforgiving Servant. Jesus made this comparison in Matthew 18: 23-35.

"Therefore, the kingdom of heaven is like a king who wanted to settle accounts with his servants. As he began the settlement, a man who owed him ten thousand bags of gold was brought to him. Since he was not able to pay, the master ordered that he and his wife and his children and all that he had be sold to repay the debt.

"At this the servant fell on his knees before him. 'Be patient with me,' he begged, 'and I will pay back everything.' The servant's master took pity on him, canceled the debt and let him go.

"But when that servant went out, he found one of his fellow servants who owed him a hundred silver coins. He grabbed him and began to choke him. 'Pay back what you owe me!' he demanded.

"His fellow servant fell to his knees and begged him, 'Be patient with me, and I will pay it back.'

"But he refused. Instead, he went off and had the man thrown into prison until he could pay the debt. When the other servants saw what had happened, they were outraged and went and told their master everything that had happened.

"Then the master called the servant in. 'You wicked servant,' he said, 'I canceled all that debt of yours because you begged me to. Shouldn't you have had mercy on your fellow servant just as I had on you?' In anger his master handed him over to the jailers to be tortured, until he should pay back all he owed.

"This is how my heavenly Father will treat each of you unless you forgive your brother or sister from your heart."

William Barclay analyzed this passage in this way:

One of the faults of the unforgiving servant was that he demanded standards from others which he was not prepared to fulfill himself. Of all human faults, this is the most common. We are, for instance, often very critical of others and very easy with ourselves...What is candid frankness in us is discourteous brutality of speech in others. What is selfishness in others is standing on our indisputable rights in our own case. What is meanness in others is thrift in ourselves. Should we fail in anything we produce half a dozen valid reasons which in others would be feeble excuses. [17]

"Of all human faults, this is the most common." Oh! So, I'm not alone in being comfortable with my sin while judging others for their sin?

Taken together, we can see that the adulterous woman and the Pharisees are not so very different. They occupy flip sides of the human sin / forgiveness coin.

- In the woman's case, she was aware of her sin and had been offered forgiveness, though she had not yet repented.
- In the Pharisees' case, Jesus had to remind them of their sin, and they silently exited, still needing to repent and be forgiven.

Sin is the common human condition; repentance and forgiveness comprise the common divine solution.

Kay Hall points out that redemption, emerging from repentance and grace, is the final step of salvation.

> To redeem is to cash in on what you have been given through the cross. You turn in your sin for your salvation. You redeem the old you for the new you.[18]

Why Are We So Judgmental?

In a 2007 survey of people ages 16-29 in the United States, nearly 90% identified Christians as judgmental. [19] What's interesting is that the survey surely contained a good percentage of Christians within it! Hence, even a too-high number of young Christians see Christians as judgmental.

First, let's acknowledge that being judgmental is rooted in human nature. Here are a few of the reasons psychologists have identified.

- Avoidance – People judge others to avoid reckoning with potential feelings of inferiority and shame. Since judging others can never give a person what they really need, they feel like they have to keep doing it. [20]
- Projection – More often than not, we are bothered by the qualities of others that we choose not to see in ourselves. We ridicule, judge and shame another's habits, appearance or lifestyle choices because they are the very ones we dislike in ourselves. [21]

- <u>Control</u> – Judging and criticizing others can also give the illusion of control. That is, if you are able to tell someone what's wrong with them, you not only think you see more than they do, you might also imagine that your criticism will cause them to change their ways. [22]

Beyond psychological reasons, there may be religious reasons for us to judge others. We may feel that we need to point out sin and call others into accountability.

There is one big problem with that. A log-sized problem.

Jesus didn't order us to judge others. In fact, he ordered the opposite in Matthew 7: 1-5.

"Do not judge, or you too will be judged. For in the same way you judge others, you will be judged, and with the measure you use, it will be measured to you.

"Why do you look at the speck of sawdust in your brother's eye and pay no attention to the plank in your own eye? How can you say to your brother, 'Let me take the speck out of your eye,' when all the time there is a plank in your own eye? You hypocrite, first take the plank out of your own eye, and then you will see clearly to remove the speck from your brother's eye."

Some translations use "log" instead of "plank." (I like the log picture above, as the colors of the log resemble an eye with the darker iris in the center.)

It's obvious that Jesus wants us to address the magnitude of our own sins before we nitpick the personal, specific sins of others. But there's another factor at work. If you were to remove a speck from someone's eye, would you go in full speed and dig around with your finger? No, you would take a very gentle, careful approach to removing the speck. If we are ever going to say something about another's sin, it should be done with gentleness and care.

The Trust Zone for Sins and Stones

I hope I've clearly established that most, if not all, of us have a comfort zone that contains twin perils. We are comfortable with our own sin, and we are judgmental toward the sin of others. We somehow feel that we have earned the right to judge others, although that right truly belongs to Jesus, and there's only a hint that we are allowed to gently correct others once we've done some detailed extraction of our own sin.

Amazingly, we do not trust that Jesus can do his job. Our attitude can be that the Holy Spirit's work is not enough. It's up to us to rush in to point out and correct the flaws of others.

What is the way forward? Where is the trust zone?

We cannot release our sins and stones without Jesus' help.

We can't immediately cleanse ourselves of our sin. Through a process of repentance, we admit what we've done wrong; through a process of forgiveness, we are washed clean of our sin. Our Lord helps us in our weakness.

We must trust that our stones are not needed. We let go of our stones labeled with the words Avoidance, Projection, and Control.

We agree that the final arbiter of others is Jesus, not us. We're assigned the role of dispensing mercy according to the mercy we've received, as seen in the Parable of the Unforgiving Servant.

Ultimately, this means that we trust Jesus to do his job, and we follow his will to do ours.

Summary of "Releasing Your Sins and Stones"

Big Thought:
We need to get uncomfortable with our sin so that we repent and receive mercy. We then share that mercy with others.

Core Passage:
John 8: 2-11

Key verse: When they kept on questioning him, he straightened up and said to them, "Let any one of you who is without sin be the first to throw a stone at her."

The Comfort Zone:
Being so comfortable with our own sin that we are comfortable in judging others.

The Trust Zone:
Trusting Jesus to do his job of judgment and grace, and following his will to do our job of dispensing mercy.

Looking at Jesus Rather Than Obstacles

What have been the biggest crises in your life?

I reviewed several of mine in my book and video study, *The Next Thing: A Christian Model for Dealing with Crises in Personal Life*. Among them were:

- The unveiling of my wife Sara's depression through her first of ten suicide attempts.
- A problem pregnancy and delivery that fortunately succeeded, but also dealing with the aftermath over the next year-and-a-half.
- Unemployment and underemployment of five years, four months over a ten-year period from 2006 to 2016.
- Caregiving for my mother in her final months of life.

Sometimes I wonder how I made it through these crises with my sanity, my health, and my marriage intact. I know one way: I clung to Jesus for dear life.

That's what Peter had to do when he encountered a crisis while walking on the Sea of Galilee with Jesus.

How Not to Handle a Crisis

In *The Next Thing*, I describe several ways in which we don't handle crisis well.

- <u>We don't acknowledge the crisis</u>. It's hard to manage a crisis when you don't accept that you are in one. Pivoting quickly into crisis response mode is essential.
- <u>We make things complicated</u>. We tend to fret about every possible outcome rather than focusing on the next thing in front of us. We don't make things easy on ourselves by clearing our calendars or reducing our own and others' expectations of what we can accomplish during this time.
- <u>We don't rest</u>. During a period when physical, mental, emotional, and spiritual rest is imperative, we run ourselves into the ground.
- <u>We don't trust God</u>. We may *say* we trust God, but in reality, we don't. We don't trust God's presence, God's peace, or God's reclaiming power to make good come out of bad. We don't trust the people God sends to us, like the old joke about the man in the flood who turned down rescue efforts because "God will provide," when God had sent two boats and a helicopter!

In a crisis, we can become too focused on getting things back to normal instead of realizing that we must walk through a crisis a step at a time (a mistake I made too often). A crisis must unfold and take its course. Twisting in the trap only makes us more stuck.

We get very focused on the obstacles presented in a crisis. We also crave a return to the safety and good feeling of our comfort zone.

Two Stories in One

Let's take a look now at the aforementioned "Walking on Water" passage from Matthew 14: 22-33. The passage begins right after the Feeding of the 5,000 story; the disciples have just collected the leftover bread and fish from the feeding.

Immediately Jesus made the disciples get into the boat and go on ahead of him to the other side, while he dismissed the crowd. After he had dismissed them, he went up on a mountainside by himself to pray. Later that night, he was there alone, and the boat was already a considerable distance from land, buffeted by the waves because the wind was against it.

Shortly before dawn Jesus went out to them, walking on the lake. When the disciples saw him walking on the lake, they were terrified. "It's a ghost," they said, and cried out in fear.

But Jesus immediately said to them: "Take courage! It is I. Don't be afraid."

"Lord, if it's you," Peter replied, "tell me to come to you on the water."

"Come," he said.

[23] Then Peter got down out of the boat, walked on the water and came toward Jesus. But when he saw the wind, he was afraid and, beginning to sink, cried out, "Lord, save me!"

Immediately Jesus reached out his hand and caught him. "You of little faith," he said, "why did you doubt?"

And when they climbed into the boat, the wind died down. Then those who were in the boat worshiped him, saying, "Truly you are the Son of God."

To me, the passage contains two stories in one. One speaks to the difficulty in rowing the boat in the face of the storm. The other describes Peter's experience walking on the water.

I want to address both stories as I break down the passage to reveal the comfort zones and the trust zones.

Two Mistakes, Three Acts of Providence

[24] The story contains two mistakes by the disciples. The obvious one is that Peter loses focus after he succeeds in walking on the water and begins to sink. The second is that the other 11 disciples have no interest in getting out on the water: they're staying in the boat! The mighty wind was slowing their progress; Jesus has mi-

raculously strolled out to them, ghost-like in the dark, across the top of the lake; and now Peter is wandering around on the waves, too! The whole experience has them frightened.

Jesus provides three acts of providence, three signs of God's care, to these trembling, exhausted men.

First, Jesus **came to them** when things went against them. In the midst of the storm, Jesus presents himself and eventually calms the storm as he enters the boat.

Second, Jesus **comforts** the disciples, saying, "Take courage! It is I. Don't be afraid." When heaven intersects earth in the Bible, we hear this assurance to release our fear, such as when the angel Gabriel appears to Mary, when the angel greets the women visiting Jesus' empty tomb, and when Jesus appears to the disciples behind locked doors.

Third, Jesus **reaches out and saves Peter** at his moment of highest distress. Jesus didn't tell Peter to come out on the water without intending to provide support when needed.

The Story's Comfort and Trust Zones

Any one of us would feel more comfortable in the boat than in the water. That was the case with the disciples.

A crisis, though, can rock our boat, much like the storm did. Or it can even overturn the boat, dumping us into unknown waters.

Whether we're in or out of the boat, our tendency is to focus on the obstacles, the problems, the threats. The disciples were very focused on the wind pushing back on their efforts and on the menacing waves that grew with the wind. Peter's attention was drawn to the waves lapping up against his legs.

But think about when Peter was successful. His main purpose was to get to Jesus. His eyes focused on Jesus.

When Peter looked at Jesus, he was able to walk on water.

One of my favorite passages in the Old Testament (and indeed, it is the theme passage for Cecil Taylor Ministries) is in 2 Chronicles 20. Enemy nations have banded together to attack Judah. God's people are outnumbered. King Jehoshaphat calls the people together to pray, then ends that prayer by saying:

We do not know what to do, but our eyes are upon you.

From Comfort Zone to Trust Zone

The Spirit of the Lord then fills one of the people, Jahaziel, who prophesies how God will win the battle and what the people are supposed to do.

This is how it was when Peter walked on water. He didn't know how to walk on water; how would you even begin? What do you step down upon? How do you push off for your next step? How do you balance on waves without a surfboard?

Peter's focus wasn't on mechanics; it was on getting to Jesus, with his eyes fixated on Christ.

When we are in trouble or in crisis, what do we do? Like I said earlier, we tend to freak out. We don't do the things we need to do to help ourselves. Ultimately, we don't trust God enough to get us through. Our eyes are not on Jesus, who helps us walk on water in the storm. Our eyes are not on God, who rescues us when the enemy is approaching. We may say we trust God, but our actions betray us.

Staying in the boat, protecting themselves, huddling in fear, focusing on the dangers and obstacles – strangely enough, that was the disciples' comfort zone. Peter exceeded that comfort zone, but then fell back into old habits when he too focused on dangers and obstacles, which caused him to sink.

When our eyes are on Jesus, we are in the trust zone. Perhaps the solution will come to us in crisis as it did with Jahaziel of Judah, but if not, we can cling to Jesus.

I can imagine Peter actually reaching Jesus, embracing him, and walking back across the water to the boat with him. Peter's total focus would have to be on Jesus, not becoming distracted by obstacles. They would have stepped back into the boat together, Jesus would have calmed the storm, and Peter would have the security of knowing that Jesus indeed took care of him all the way through this event.

Jesus is ready to do the same, to walk on the water with you, side by side. He will come to you, comfort you, and reach out to save you. But the trust trick is to look in his eyes, focus on him, and believe in him, not getting distracted by your obstacles. He will protect your soul, regardless of the outcome of the crisis.

Summary of "Looking at Jesus Rather Than Obstacles"

Big Thought:
Instead of denying crisis is happening or focusing on the obstacles surrounding you, focus on looking at and clinging to Jesus while in crisis.

Core Passage:
Matthew 14: 22-33

Key verse: But when *(Peter)* saw the wind, he was afraid and, beginning to sink, cried out, "Lord, save me!" Immediately Jesus reached out his hand and caught him. "You of little faith," he said, "why did you doubt?"

The Comfort Zone:
Focusing on overcoming obstacles so we can return to normal as quickly as possible.

The Trust Zone:
Keeping our eyes on Jesus and relying on him to be a very present help in times of trouble.

Exchanging the Familiar for a New Calling

Much like the title of this chapter, I want to exchange a familiar Gospel story's meaning for an additional interpretation.

The time is post-Resurrection. The disciples have been through a trying time in Jerusalem. They have returned to Galilee. Seven of them are together when Peter suddenly says, "I'm going fishing," and off they go to the boat for an all-night expedition on the Sea of Galilee.

Why does Peter want to go fishing? The Bible gives no explanation, so I'll speculate. I feel like Peter wanted to get into his comfort zone. He had fished all of his life. Now that he's been through such stress with Jesus' death and resurrection, it's natural that fishing would be a relaxing activity. I don't think it was Peter going backward in his obligations to Christ, rather that he was looking to unwind.

The fishing didn't go well, according to the Gospel story. As dawn breaks, Jesus appears on the shore and instructs the disciples to throw their net on the other side. As they bring in a haul of 153 fish, they realize it's their resurrected Savior standing on the shore. Peter dives out of the boat to swim to Jesus, while the others arrive later, dragging the fish, just in time for a breakfast Jesus has prepared.

Now we reach a part of the story that is entitled "Jesus Reinstates Peter" in your Bible. It's found in John 21: 15-19.

²⁵ When they had finished eating, Jesus said to Simon Peter, "Simon son of John, do you love me more than these?"

"Yes, Lord," he said, "you know that I love you."

Jesus said, "Feed my lambs."

Again Jesus said, "Simon son of John, do you love me?"
He answered, "Yes, Lord, you know that I love you."
Jesus said, "Take care of my sheep."

The third time he said to him, "Simon son of John, do you love me?"

Peter was hurt because Jesus asked him the third time, "Do you love me?" He said, "Lord, you know all things; you know that I love you."

Jesus said, "Feed my sheep. Very truly I tell you, when you were younger you dressed yourself and went where you wanted; but when you are old you will stretch out your hands, and someone else will dress you and lead you where you do not want to go." Jesus said this to indicate the kind of death by which Peter would glorify God. Then he said to him, "Follow me!"

This is traditionally known as the Reinstatement of Peter because, just as Peter denied Jesus three times after his arrest, so Jesus asks for three apologies or affirmations from Peter. Very symbolic.

But I think there's another symbolism in the story that we miss if we stop there.

Once a Fisherman, Now a Shepherd

[26] The Synoptic Gospels (Matthew, Mark, Luke) tell a different story than the Gospel of John regarding Peter's initial call. In the Synoptic version, Jesus walks along the same Sea of Galilee shoreline, scooping up future disciples Peter and Andrew, and James and John soon after. Here's the version in Matthew 4: 18-20.

> As Jesus was walking beside the Sea of Galilee, he saw two brothers, Simon called Peter and his brother Andrew. They were casting a net into the lake, for they were fishermen. "Come, follow me," Jesus said, "and I will send you out to fish for people." At once they left their nets and followed him.

Jesus explains the mission in a way that Peter and Andrew can understand. They are now evangelists, following Jesus and helping him bring people into his ministry.

Over time, Peter surely had gotten comfortable with following Jesus and becoming the lead disciple. His role evolved into a comfort zone.

But now, Jesus needs to push Peter to a new role, as the lead shepherd in his absence.

It's one thing to reel in people for Christ; it's another thing to shepherd, guide, protect, and love them. Peter has already heard the job description, as outlined by Jesus describing himself in John 10: 14-17.

> "I am the good shepherd; I know my sheep and my sheep know me—just as the Father knows me and I know the Father—and I lay down my life for the sheep. I have other sheep that are not of this sheep pen. I must bring them also. They too will listen to my voice, and there shall be one flock and one shepherd. The reason my Father loves me is that I lay down my life—only to take it up again."

Now, I'm not saying that Peter is THE good shepherd; that role is always Christ's. But Jesus does need a trusted, earthly shepherd to lead his flock and to gather the other sheep (Gentiles) not currently in his sheep pen, to create one flock with one shepherd leader.

With a conversion from fisher of people to shepherd of people, Peter is asked to go deeper, with greater love and sacrifice. In fact, in the two passages we've read, there is the undertone that Peter the Shepherd will also lay down his life for the sheep, as Jesus outlined in the reinstatement passage.

The key point to make here is that Peter entered a trust zone to become a disciple in the first place. That trust zone became a comfort zone over time. Now Peter is assigned to a new trust zone as shepherd.

The same happens for us. We leave our comfort zones for trust zones. Iteratively, we do it again and again, as the trust zone becomes a comfort zone, and Jesus brings new assignments to us.

Surely you can reflect on your life and see this pattern. I certainly see it in mine. Here is my example of that iteration.

Two Calls

It was all set in my mind. I was going to return to my college town and work for a large, well-known computer company.

A no-brainer, it seemed. After two years of unhappiness in my post-college city, I would be surrounded by college friends I had left behind. I could keep an eye on my grandparents, to whom I had grown close during my college years. The salary offer was good, and the opportunities for a long career with this company were promising.

To put it in terms of this book, I was returning to my comfort zone.

Still, I figured I really ought to pray about a big decision like this, even if I knew the answer already. Hadn't God set all this up for me?

My response to the company was due Friday. On Tuesday, I prayed, confident that God would affirm my choice. Then in prayer, I heard a voice:

"That youth group needs you."

What? There must be some mistake.

And not only because the Spirit's response was misaligned with my plans for my comfort zone reunion. But the youth group?

I had started volunteering with my church's youth group a few months prior to this prayer. My impact on them: Zero. I was so scrawny and young-looking that the teens thought I was another member of their group! Even though I had been a leader in my high school youth group, I couldn't seem to find any traction in building relationships or executing any notable tasks. I was just sort of there, seemingly in the corner.

God telling me that the youth group needed me seemed like crossed wires. Perhaps I misheard. Perhaps I imagined the voice. I would try again on Wednesday.

But the next day and the day after that, I heard the same voice and the same message during prayer: "That youth group needs you." Deep breath. Frown. Sigh of resignation. There must be something to this.

Friday came, and I reluctantly called the company representative and declined the offer. How would I explain this to my friends? That God told me not to come back? I landed on telling them that I felt like I hadn't given my new city enough of a chance. And I entered the trust zone, not knowing what lay ahead.

Eugene, another young male sponsor, sat with me in the youth room for adult sync-up that Sunday evening, awaiting the volunteer couple that led the program at our small church. The couple finally walked in and announced, "We're burned out. We're quitting immediately. You're in charge now." And they spun and walked out.

Wow! The Lord could see farther ahead than me. That youth group really did need me!

For the next eight months, while the church searched for a youth pastor, Eugene and I led the youth program. It was tremendous fun. We tried creative ideas that mostly worked. We got close to the teens, who appreciated that we were there for them when the leaders left. That was the start of my 30-year mission in youth work, one of the greatest blessings of my life.

And my comfort zone. One I didn't want to give up, obviously, if I stuck around for 30 years!

God had another mission in mind: Cecil Taylor Ministries. Once I had decided to go forward with this ministry, I continued my normal high volunteer workload. But God started urging me to peel away other obligations in order to focus on the ministry.

The volunteer arena that I argued the most to retain was youth ministry, my great love. I had never gotten tired of working with youth. But finally, I gave that up, too. I was committed to a new trust zone with this ministry to go beyond the walls of my church and teach Christians how to live a 7-day practical faith. It's why you're reading this book right now.

How Do You Recognize Your Call?

These aforementioned calls came to me in different ways. The first was spectacular, a lightning moment during prayer. The second also came during prayer, but as more of a persistent nudge, a recurring thought, that played out over months of prayer.

There are other ways to recognize your call. It could be from conscience or from the voices of other people, speaking truth into your life. I've had that kind of direction many times.

A little trickier to discern is how the Lord works through what's going on in your life. One method is through the events of your life. As things happen in life, you may find yourself headed in a new direction. A job loss might open you up to new alternatives. An injury or illness might change your priorities. Pay attention as you go through life changes to discern if the Lord is using this event (not causing the event but using it) to steer you in another direction.

A second method to ponder is when you feel your passions changing. This could be a sign to go a new direction. You may feel less enthusiasm for some venture or venue. You may feel stimulated by something that is new to you. I'm going through one of those cycles right now that indicates it's time to shake up a particular part of my life. When your passions change, it can be both disturbing and exhilarating to seek a call in a new direction.

God is looking for kingdom risktakers. Is it your time to take a risk? Is it necessary for you to outgrow your comfort zone? Is it your moment to exchange the familiar for a new calling?

Summary of "Exchanging the Familiar for a New Calling"

Big Thought:
God possesses the vision to steer you in new, fruitful directions when you are faithful to his call.

Core Passage:
John 21: 15-19

Key verse: Again Jesus said, "Simon son of John, do you love me?" He answered, "Yes, Lord, you know that I love you." Jesus said, "Take care of my sheep."

The Comfort Zone:
A trust zone that has become a comfort zone over time.

The Trust Zone:
A new challenge to shake you out of your comfort zone and deepen your commitment to Christ.

Relinquishing Certainty, Embracing Uncertainty

I remember teaching a class of 30-somethings years ago and asking them, "What is the hardest thing about following Christ?"

The number one answer: "Giving up control."

When we answer Jesus' call, when we go all-in for Christ, we still want control of our lives. We can mentally assent to God's ways and decisions being better than ours, but in practice, we can fight God constantly for control of our lives.

When we perceive we have control, then we feel like we have achieved certainty. In reality, that is a foolish thought. It only takes the turning of one day of the calendar to discover that life is much more fragile and uncertain than we think it is.

To illustrate this point, I want to break down the Gospel stories of two men who thought they had it made. One man is fictional; the other encountered Jesus in a way that ultimately saddened him.

The Fool and His Barns

When do we have it made? How much is enough?

A survey was taken of Americans some years ago, asking "How much salary would you need to earn to think you had it made?" Here is a summary of the answers:

- For those making $25,000 per year, they saw $50,000 as the goal to "have it made."
- For those making $50,000, the ideal was $100,000.
- Those making $100,000 said $200,000.
- Those making $200,000 said $500,000.

Do you see the pattern? The consensus was that a person needed to earn at least twice as much as currently in order to feel secure and certain.

This also implies that if someone making $25,000 per year achieved a $50,000 salary, their perspective would change. The new goal would be $100,000! So, $50,000 indeed wasn't enough to satisfy them. The target always shifts. It's greed in action.

Jesus told a parable about a rich man who figured that he had finally reached the point of satisfaction, in Luke 12: 15-21.

Then (Jesus) said to them, "Watch out! Be on your guard against all kinds of greed; life does not consist in an abundance of possessions."

And he told them this parable: "The ground of a certain rich man yielded an abundant harvest. He thought to himself, 'What shall I do? I have no place to store my crops.'

"Then he said, 'This is what I'll do. I will tear down my barns and build bigger ones, and there I will store my surplus grain. And I'll say to myself, "You have plenty of grain laid up for many years. Take life easy; eat, drink and be merry."'"

"But God said to him, 'You fool! This very night your life will be demanded from you. Then who will get what you have prepared for yourself?'

"This is how it will be with whoever stores up things for themselves but is not rich toward God."

Such certainty this man had! He had it all figured out. But God lets us know that such certainty is not part of the life we have on earth. Certainty only comes from reliance on God; hence, when we build our barns and add to their supply, those barns should be built on the foundation of Jesus.

The Rich Man's Disappointment

The fool was fictional; the next rich man was not.

Jesus encountered an earnest man who wanted to know more about eternal life and how to qualify. There are three versions of this story in the Synoptic gospels; I've chosen the one in Mark 10: 17-22.

As Jesus started on his way, a man ran up to him and fell on his knees before him. "Good teacher," he asked, "what must I do to inherit eternal life?"

"Why do you call me good?" Jesus answered. "No one is good—except God alone. You know the commandments: 'You shall not murder, you shall not commit adultery, you shall not steal, you shall not give false testimony, you shall not defraud, honor your father and mother.'"

"Teacher," he declared, "all these I have kept since I was a boy."

[27] Jesus looked at him and loved him. "One thing you lack," he said. "Go, sell everything you have and give to the poor, and you will have treasure in heaven. Then come, follow me."

At this the man's face fell. He went away sad, because he had great wealth.

This man is described elsewhere as a rich young man or a rich young ruler. In either case, he probably had inherited a great sum of money; still, he was clearly ethical. He had not stolen or lied his way forward. He had not defrauded anyone. He had been obedient to an ethical, religious life but somehow realized that it wasn't enough.

I selected Mark's story, as it's the only version that indicates how Jesus loved him. Christ saw into the young ruler's heart and loved most of what he saw. Jesus realized that not only did the young man have strong religious principles and had potential to be a better follower, but he also saw the man's weak spot – his comfort zone. It was his wealth.

Jesus followed this encounter by discussing how hard it is for the rich to enter the kingdom of heaven, uttering his famous line about how it's easier for a camel to go through the eye of a needle than for the rich to enter the kingdom.

As we look at these stories of the rich fool and the rich young ruler, it's easy to chalk up their mistakes to greed. But I think there is a deeper meaning than simple greed, in both of their cases.

Our Quest for Certainty

What does wealth bring you? Our answers might be possessions, social standing, even options – we love having options. But the other thing wealth **seems** to bring you is certainty.

My family and I have oscillated between having money and not having money. I grew up wearing my taller best friend's hand-me-downs in high school. I've had tens of thousands in credit card debt pile up because I was out of work for more than a year. I've also had enough money in the bank account to not worry too much about what I was spending. And we went back and forth between the two extremes; I worked for decades in high tech, where you were either working lots of overtime because the company was booming, or you were laid off because the company was busting.

In my experience, the biggest difference in those two states of wealth is certainty. When you are impoverished, things are very uncertain. You don't know what's going to happen or how you will handle it. It feels like the wolves are at your door. It feels like if you defend one door, then they will penetrate the other door. Life on the edge is full of uncertainty.

When you have money and options, it's a different feeling. You have more certainty. You don't worry about whether the check is going to bounce; you know that it won't.

Going Beyond Money

I want to emphasize that I'm using money as an example, but that's not the main topic here. The theme is certainty vs. uncertainty, and what it means to comfort zones and trust zones.

People crave certainty; it's natural, in an uncertain world, to desire certainty. People can find certainty in different ways.

Someone reading this book loves their **routine**. They enjoy having that certainty of each day's schedule. They rely on it. They get off track if their routine is disrupted.

Someone reading this book (along with the one writing it!) loves their **to-do list**. Yes, a to-do list is a great organizational idea, but does it go beyond planning to obsession?

Someone reading this book doesn't like **surprises**. They will go out of their way to not be surprised. They simply don't adapt well to the unexpected. Don't throw them a surprise party!

Someone reading this book has their life **all planned out**. At a certain age, they will marry. At another age, they will have children. They know how many children they will have. They have an idea of when and where they will retire. Can I tell you all the ways that these plans could go sideways?

What lengths will we pursue in order to achieve certainty in an uncertain world?

A Tolerance for Ambiguity

A great follow-up question is, **how will we reorient ourselves to deal better with uncertainty?**

Before he owned the Dallas Cowboys football team, Jerry Jones made his millions as a wildcatter who would find oil by drilling between dry holes. He came to see business, and other aspects of life, as a risky venture. Jones once said:

> "I have a very high tolerance for ambiguity. A low tolerance for ambiguity is when somebody has to know that weekly check is going to be there on Friday or they're not a good functioning person. It worries them too much. On the other hand, some people are at their very best when they don't know what's going to be there." [28]

For the Christian, dealing with ambiguity and uncertainty is part of following Jesus.

- He never promises us wealth; instead, Jesus points out that he doesn't have a place to lay his own head.
- Jesus doesn't promise that every prayer will be answered as we wish, but he does promise that God listens constantly and will respond in a loving way, according to God's will.
- As we've seen, Jesus doesn't promise us control or certainty; he simply instructs his disciples, "Follow me!"

I've told this story in another book, but it bears repeating. There was a time when I had left one job and was out of work, looking for another. People within my industry assured me that I would certainly find work within six months.

Well, the six-month mark came, and there was no job offer in sight. My prayers turned panicky, asking God where I was being led and how soon it could happen.

After a few of these, I suppose God had heard enough. In prayer, I felt this response: "You worry too much. I want you to just follow me, daily."

With the Holy Spirit's relentless help, I started following Jesus more closely each day and quit worrying so much about outcomes. I embraced uncertainty and stopped panic-praying.

It took another five months for me to find a part-time job and another five months after that to find a full-time job. But one momentous thing that happened during that window of time was that I felt the call to found Cecil Taylor Ministries. It didn't happen right away; it took months to develop the ministry as a side venture and years for me to finally quit my job and take a leap of faith into the uncertain realm of creating a ministry from scratch.

I'm not saying everyone has to quit their job or sell all that they have in order to follow God; not everyone has those particular calls. But I do believe everyone has a call to embrace uncertainty, even while following the most certain, constant force in the universe, our Lord.

Trusting through Uncertainty

Let's take a fresh look at the rich young man who didn't want to give up his wealth. No doubt, Jesus wanted him to be generous. But even more, Jesus wanted him to give up something precious in order to follow more closely – his certainty. By trading his wealth, the young man would have entered a trust zone of uncertainty where he would find a new certainty of spirit under the care of Christ.

And what about the fool and his barns? He not only had certainty figured out, but he felt no need for God. He had certainty in the bag – or in the barn. But his life was required of him, so reliance on God should have been the goal.

All of us can fall into the comfort zone trap of relying on something that seems to create certainty. Maybe we're so close to that comfort zone that we can't even see it anymore.

John Rabins says we make the mistake of equating "uncomfortable" with "unbearable." [29] That distinction reminds me of another rich young ruler: Cuzco in the Disney movie, "The Emperor's New Groove." He craved certainty in a selfish way but lost it all when magically turned into a llama. Given a second chance at palace life as a human, he ultimately found another kind of certainty, relying on relationships rather than power.

Our trust zone is giving up the certainty we create for ourselves by embracing the uncertainty that comes from a relationship with God. The relationship itself is sound and certain and leads to eternal life. But the details feel risky at times. We don't know where God will lead us, and we don't know how life will treat us, so we ideally come to rely on him fully.

Relinquishing Certainty, Embracing Uncertainty

In Luke 9:24-25, Jesus says:

"For whoever wants to save their life will lose it, but whoever loses their life for me will save it. What good is it for someone to gain the whole world, and yet lose or forfeit their very self?"

Losing your life for Christ? Sounds very uncertain.

But uncertainty is the soil in which faith grows.

Summary of "Relinquishing Certainty, Embracing Uncertainty"

Big Thought:
We crave for our passage in life to be full of certainty. But Jesus draws us to a life that is rife with uncertainty, except for the certainty of his presence, love, and salvation.

Core Passage:
Mark 10: 17-22

Key verse: "One thing you lack," he said. "Go, sell everything you have and give to the poor, and you will have treasure in heaven. Then come, follow me."

The Comfort Zone:
Our quest for certainty through earthly means in a scary, uncertain world.

The Trust Zone:
Embracing ambiguity and uncertainty in your life while leaning on Jesus for your certainty.

Trading Governments and Empires for Jesus' Kingdom

A subset of Jesus' disciples was vastly disappointed in him. These men wanted more. They wanted a political Messiah who would liberate the land from Roman rule.

This group consisted of Judas Iscariot, Simon the Zealot, James the son of Alphaeus, and a fourth disciple who went by a number of names:

- In the Gospel of Mark, he's called Thaddeus.
- In Luke and the Acts of the Apostles, he's known as Judas the son of James.
- In John, he is simply Judas.
- In Matthew, he is labeled as Lebbaeus whose surname was Thaddeus.
- For our purposes, we'll use **Thaddeus**.

Only once do we hear Thaddeus' voice in scripture: At the Last Supper, when he asked Jesus a question. The exchange comes in John 14: 22-24.

> Then Judas (not Judas Iscariot) said, "But, Lord, why do you intend to show yourself to us and not to the world?"

Jesus replied, "Anyone who loves me will obey my teaching. My Father will love them, and we will come to them and make our home with them. Anyone who does not love me will not obey my teaching. These words you hear are not my own; they belong to the Father who sent me."

Jesus was well aware he was dealing with a Jewish Zealot, one of four in his inner circle of disciples. This group arose from an uprising that occurred around the time of Jesus' birth.

When Herod the Great died, and his kingdom was divided among four rulers, including his son Herod Antipas in Galilee, Palestine erupted. A man named Judas the Galilean raised an insurrection, stormed the palace of Sepphoris, armed his followers from its arsenal, and embarked on a revolution. Roman power speedily broke Judas the Galilean's revolt, but it was directly from him that the Zealots stemmed.[30]

Judas the Galilean made a second run at revolt in the year 6 after the Judean governor, Quirinius, instituted a new census aimed at taxation. To pay taxes to Rome was an offense to Jews who believed that tribute could only be paid to God, and another insurrection took place. Judas the Galilean was killed in this affair.

The first century historian Josephus wrote this about the Zealots:

> They have an inviolable attachment to liberty and say that God is their only Ruler and Lord. They do not mind dying any kind of death, nor do they heed the torture of their kindred and their friends, nor can any such fear make them call any man lord.[31]

In summary, the Zealots were religious people who had political aims in mind and were willing to resort to any means, including violence, to achieve them.

Jesus' Answer to Thaddeus' Question

Thus, when Thaddeus asked his question, Jesus understood the context. He sensed that Thaddeus really wanted to know why Jesus would not publicly reveal that he was a political Messiah and get the crowds under his control. Jesus knew the message underlying Thaddeus' question was, why will Jesus not seize the moment to usher in a new political regime?

So, Jesus didn't directly answer the question. Instead, Christ pointed to his desire to win hearts, not by forcing his control over crowds, but by gently making a home with individuals.

J. Ellsworth Kalas writes in The Thirteen Apostles:

> With those few words, Jesus stated the operating principle of his kingdom. It is a kingdom of love…Jesus explained that a person cannot be forced into discipleship…This is a correction for so many of our missionary and evangelistic endeavors. Constantine and a good many later military and government leaders believed they could make Christians by force.[32]

Thaddeus' question was a last plea to align Jesus with the goals of the Zealots. They had followed him for these three years of discipleship, waiting for their moment.

The Heinous Coin

Jesus must have really frustrated the Zealots two days earlier, a moment that seems clearer and more poignant now that we understand the Zealot background. The story is recorded in Matthew 22: 15-22.

Then the Pharisees went out and laid plans to trap him in his words. They sent their disciples to him along with the Herodians. "Teacher," they said, "we know that you are a man of integrity and that you teach the way of God in accordance with the truth. You aren't swayed by others, because you pay no attention to who they are. Tell us then, what is your opinion? Is it right to pay the imperial tax to Caesar or not?"

[33] But Jesus, knowing their evil intent, said, "You hypocrites, why are you trying to trap me? Show me the coin used for paying the tax." They brought him a denarius, and he asked them, "Whose image is this? And whose inscription?"

"Caesar's," they replied.

Then he said to them, "So give back to Caesar what is Caesar's, and to God what is God's."

When they heard this, they were amazed. So they left him and went away.

Usually we take this passage on a surface level, pointing to Jesus' clever ability to foil the Pharisees and their strange bedfellows, the Herodians.[ii] But there's another level. Let's look again at that coin that was handed to Jesus.

---

ii   The Herodians were Jews that supported Roman rule. If Jesus had said anything against the tribute, the Herodians would have surely reported his treason to the Roman governor. If Jesus had supported the tribute, the Pharisees would have pronounced Jesus as disloyal to the Jewish nation

[34] On one side was the portrait of Emperor Tiberius. On the other side was this inscription in Latin: "Tiberius Caesar Augustus, son of the divine Augustus."

Realize this stunning fact: Jesus was holding a coin that described Tiberius in the same terms Jesus described himself: As a Son of the Divine!

That means Jesus was holding an image of a false idol.

He might as well have been holding a coin showing Baal from the Old Testament: a false god.

Jesus could have been offended by this coin. He could have launched into a speech about false idols represented on coins. He could have condemned a Roman government that set up its emperors as more than men, as gods, as they ruled over the Promised Land of the one true God. Using his miraculous power, he could have melted the idolatrous coin in his hand or turned it to metal fragments.

This was a moment when Thaddeus might have caught his breath, wondering if Jesus would finally reveal himself. This was a moment when Jesus could declare that *he* was the rightful king of this land. In his righteous anger at being handed the coin referring to a false god, Christ could have declared holy war on the Roman Empire in that very moment.

Instead, Jesus focused on the trick the Pharisees and Herodians wanted to play on him. He simply handed the coin back to the giver. He had no interest in the occupying government or in overthrowing it.

Why, Thaddeus must have wondered, like we might wonder as well? Why would Jesus have little interest in becoming an earthly king over the land? Or even stating a firm opinion about Roman occupation?

Jesus' Priority

With an eternal perspective, Jesus knew that governments, empires, and dictators rise and fall. As I write this, Vladimir Putin is the global bad guy. He'll be gone someday. Autocrats eventually die off, if they are not overthrown.

Empires and dynasties have risen and fallen, before and after Jesus's time on earth. Kings and queens were once powerful rulers, but in our time, they have mostly been reduced to figureheads.

In my country, the United States, a Republican will win the presidency one time, a Democrat the next. Congressional majorities will shift back and forth between one party or the other. The politicians and their parties cycle in and out. The same goes for multi-party democracies the world over. Laws will be made, overturned, and reinstated over the decades.

What lasts is the eternal – what belongs to God.

Moreover, Jesus had a different kingdom in mind. Not one that rules the land, but one, like he told Thaddeus, that rules the heart.

Jesus craves our hearts. He came to win our souls, to show us how to live righteously, to spread his compassion and love for our fellow people so that we would love them, too. Jesus wants to abide within us, at one with the Father within our souls. Once that happens, we ideally would act in ways that represent Jesus' priorities in all worldly affairs.

It's distressing to see how we Christians have become distracted from following Jesus' priorities and teaching. Russell Moore, editor-in-chief of "Christianity Today", said during an interview aired on NPR's *All Things Considered* in August 2023:

> Multiple pastors tell me, essentially, the same story about quoting the Sermon on the Mount, parenthetically, in their preaching—'turn the other cheek'—[and] to have someone come up after to [complain]…When the pastor would say, 'I'm literally quoting Jesus Christ' ... The response would be, 'Yes, but that doesn't work anymore. That's weak.' [35]

As Christians, we need to make sure our primary goal is to follow what Jesus says. As he demonstrates in the exchange with Thaddeus, Jesus' foremost priority is to win the heart of an individual.

But on the Other Hand…

I realize a good question is, how are we Christians supposed to engage with governments and politics? What is the "sweet spot" between full political focus and attending solely to the spiritual? Sometimes it's necessary to engage in politics and governments, right? Doesn't God have some priorities that can only become manifest through governmental action?

For example, the Bible instructs us to engage within the **judicial** system to plead for the oppressed in our society (Isaiah 1: 17).

> Learn to do right; seek justice.
> Defend the oppressed.
> Take up the cause of the fatherless;
> plead the case of the widow.

Isaiah later goes further to warn those in **legislative** or **executive** roles to be just and to avoid oppressing those with least advantage (Isaiah 10: 1-2):

Woe to those who make unjust laws,
to those who issue oppressive decrees,
to deprive the poor of their rights
and withhold justice from the oppressed of my people,
making widows their prey
and robbing the fatherless.

Clearly, we are supposed to participate in government affairs. Certainly we should engage in the world and use our gifts, some of which may be useful in dealing with governments and politics. We should vote. We should follow our conscience to advocate for causes, especially Biblically-based ones as described above; those causes may require us to venture into the realm of governments and politics.

But those inevitably seem like technical details to me. Let me bring back the discussion to the essential questions we should ask ourselves:

- Where is my trust?
- Where is my belief?
- Where is my **comfort zone**?
- Where is my **trust zone**?

Trading Political Comfort Zones for Trust Zones of the Heart

How do we know when we've gone too far, like Thaddeus and the Zealots?

I've thought about this a lot. This is the conclusion I've come to.

- If you believe that a government is your rescuer;
- If you believe that one political movement will save the country and the world, and that another political movement is intolerable disaster;
- If you believe that a law will fix errant morality;
- If you believe that a politician is your leader and your savior from what troubles you;

...then you're in a comfort zone where you are placing your trust in governments and empires, and not Jesus.

Our Christ wants you to leave that worldly comfort zone and enter the trust zone of his kingdom, where the slain lamb is on the throne, where changing hearts is supremely important compared to changing laws or courts or governments.

The Pope and the Fall of Communism

You may say, "Cecil, this is ridiculous. You **have** to have politics to get things done in this world. Simply invoking Christ's name can't change the world, can it?"

Let me share the story of how invoking the name of Christ was a key moment in the fall of Soviet-based communism in the last quarter of the 20th century.

Author and *Wall Street Journal* columnist Peggy Noonan points to the moment that changed everything.

I think I know the moment Soviet communism began its fall. It happened in public. Anyone could see it. It was one of the great spiritual moments of the 20th century, maybe the greatest.

It was the first week in June 1979... John Paul II was a new pope, raised to the papacy just eight months before. The day after he became pope he made it clear he would like to return as pope to his native Poland to see his people.

The communists who ran the Polish regime faced a quandary. If they didn't allow the new Pope to return to his homeland, they would look defensive and frightened, as if they feared that he had more power than they. To rebuff him would seem an admission of their weakness. On the other hand, if they let him return, the people might rise up against the government, which might in turn trigger an invasion by the Soviet Union. [36]

Eventually the Polish communists allowed the Pope to visit Poland, calculating that he would be cautious in his approach, and the impact of his visit would fizzle.

But a week into his trip, Pope John Paul II held a mass in a field outside Krakow. It's estimated that two to three million people attended.

The Pope did not call directly for political overthrow. What he called for instead was for the spirit of Christ to reign inside the people:

I speak for Christ himself: "Receive the Holy Spirit!"...

You must be strong with the strength that faith gives!... You must be strong with love, which is stronger than death. . . . When we are strong with the Spirit of God, we are also strong with the faith of man. . . . There is therefore no need to fear. . . . So . . . I beg you: Never lose your trust, do not be defeated, do not be discouraged. . . . Always seek spiritual power from Him from whom countless generations of our fathers and mothers have found it. Never detach yourselves from Him. Never lose your spiritual freedom. [37]

Using the jargon of this book, Pope John Paul II was encouraging the Polish people to enter a trust zone based on the spiritual power of God, the Holy Spirit, to open their hearts to freely let in the Son and the Father. He didn't visit Poland to overthrow communism; he came to encourage open hearts.

Even if communism had <u>not</u> changed in any timely way, the Pope was promising that the Polish people's lives would be different because they lived in Jesus' trust zone.

This echoes Paul's advice on prayer in Philippians 4: 6-7:

> Do not be anxious about anything, but in every situation, by prayer and petition, with thanksgiving, present your requests to God. And the peace of God, which transcends all understanding, will guard your hearts and your minds in Christ Jesus.

Paul doesn't promise answered prayers. He promises peace and presence and protection for our **hearts**. That can happen even behind an iron curtain.

With Christ in our hearts, a particular political stance is not as important as the movement of the Holy Spirit within the people who serve him.

In this scheme, the heart leads; any possible political ramifications follow. Not the other way around. History shows us that a movement that changes a law without changing hearts will eventually fail or be overthrown.

Mapping Back to Thaddeus

What we learn from Thaddeus' story is that the comfort zone is our misplaced trust in governmental institutions, political parties, and political leaders. At the end of the day, these will all let you down. Yet we cling to them out of fear in an uncertain world, looking to them for our rescue and salvation.

The trust zone is the place where we render unto God what is God's – our very lives and souls – where our true Savior reigns, where there is certainty in the One who never changes, where our house is built on the rock of Jesus, where we obey Christ's teaching because we love him. We cry out for the one true Lord to save us and abide with us. The result is an intimate trust zone, where the Father and the Son make their home within our hearts.

Hearts don't change from bludgeoning them; Jesus didn't advise that in what he told Thaddeus. The heart's door must be opened from the inside by an obedient person before he and the Father enter. Then the trust zone can be established.

And then the world can be changed as hearts are changed.

How Did Thaddeus Respond?

[38] Ah, Thaddeus. Let's get back to Thaddeus and see how this political rebel responded to what Jesus told him.

After the Last Supper and Christ's arrest, crucifixion, and resurrection, we learn in Acts of the Apostles that Thaddeus stayed with the apostles and was present when Jesus ascended into heaven.

Interestingly, he and the remaining zealots did not wander off seeking another messiah to remove Roman rule. (By the way, actions of the Zealot movement eventually led to the backlash that was Roman destruction of Jerusalem in the year 70).

Instead, Thaddeus and the remaining revolutionaries were transformed into the followers their Lord was seeking. They had left their political comfort zone and entered his trust zone of the heart. They devoted their lives to building the fledgling church instead of destroying the government. According to The Apostolic Constitutions, a set of early Christian literature, Thaddeus was originally in charge of administering to widows, some of the most oppressed in Jewish society, some of the folks Isaiah insisted on protecting.

Legend has it that Thaddeus was killed by torture and finally arrows at Ararat. In doing so, he became known as Saint Jude. Yes, Thaddeus is the saint who is the namesake of a hospital for the desperate, as he is the patron saint of lost causes.

[39] Thaddeus lost *his* cause, so to speak, when he willingly gave up his comfort zone, trading governments and empires for a trust zone of higher calling, changing hearts for the Lord, and helping to reveal Jesus' eternal kingdom.

I want to make one last point about this story. Jesus brought the Zealots alongside him as disciples, knowing their political motivations, knowing they would be disappointed in his approach. Why? Because Jesus doesn't give up on anyone. He wanted to change their hearts, too. The Zealots' transformation from rebels to shepherds stands as a powerful example of what we can do as well when we take a leap of faith into Jesus' trust zone that drives us to pursue hearts instead of political power.

Summary of "Trading Governments and Empires for Jesus' Kingdom"

Big Thought:
Governments and empires will fail and fall. Take a leap of faith into the eternal kingdom of Jesus as your primary hope.

Core Passage:
John 14: 22-24

Key verse: "Anyone who loves me will obey my teaching. My Father will love them, and we will come to them and make our home with them."

Key verse from Matthew 15: 21: "Give back to Caesar what is Caesar's, and to God what is God's."

The Comfort Zone:
Reliance on governments, political parties, and political leaders to save us.

The Trust Zone:
Opening our hearts and pursuing others' hearts to serve Jesus' aim to live in those hearts.

Leaving Safety for Danger

There was a knock on the door that evening that could have changed my life. Well, it did, in a positive way. But it could have changed my life in a negative way. There was no way of knowing.

Sixteen years old and with a fresh driver's license, I was home alone in the parsonage while my preacher dad and the rest of my family were at a school function. Then someone knocked on the front door.

It wasn't unusual for people to come to the parsonage with requests; in a small town, the pastor's house is similar to the United Way. It's where you go for help.

I opened the door to a man who spoke no English. In our part of the country, that usually signaled that he was an illegal immigrant who had come across the Rio Grande from Mexico. Having taken high school Spanish for two years, I could get by in a simple conversation. The man had a simple request: Could I drive him to the next town, eight miles away?

I hesitated. This was a time when carjackings seemed on the rise; or perhaps as a new driver, I was just more aware. A few illegal immigrants were dangerous, though most just wanted to work on farms and keep their profiles low.

Then I thought, "What would my father do?" If my father were here, he would surely drive the man to the next town. So I told him to wait for me out front, and I would pull the car around.

Locking up the house, I prayed to my Heavenly Father. "Please, Lord, I want to help this man, but it feels dangerous. Please protect me."

We drove to the next town, making small talk based on my limited Spanish. I dropped him off, he thanked me, and that was it.

Driving back home, I felt a sense of both relief and accomplishment. I thought how I did what my father would have done. And I realized that I had done what my Heavenly Father would have me do; when I had asked, "What would my father do?", I could have just as easily been wondering about God through Jesus Christ, WWJD-style.

We've seen throughout the stories in this book that Jesus calls us to uncomfortable places. Sometimes we're called even to dangerous places, perhaps to be missionaries, perhaps to travel into the "bad" parts of town, perhaps to minister in prisons, perhaps to drive in a blizzard or flood to help someone. Usually the greater danger is matched by greater benefit to the kingdom.

Here's a time when Jesus called a follower into what they perceived to be a dangerous situation, but it actually wasn't – much like when I drove the man to the next town.

"Go!"

Ananias was a Christian in Damascus who was called by the Lord in a vision. Based on where this story is positioned, after Saul has been blinded by the resurrected Christ, and Ananias' comments, it can be understood that "the Lord" is also the resurrected Jesus.

Ananias was called into a potentially dangerous mission, described in Acts of the Apostles, 9: 10-19a.

In Damascus there was a disciple named Ananias. The Lord called to him in a vision, "Ananias!"

"Yes, Lord," he answered.

The Lord told him, "Go to the house of Judas on Straight Street and ask for a man from Tarsus named Saul, for he is praying. In a vision he has seen a man named Ananias come and place his hands on him to restore his sight."

"Lord," Ananias answered, "I have heard many reports about this man and all the harm he has done to your holy people in Jerusalem. And he has come here with authority from the chief priests to arrest all who call on your name."

But the Lord said to Ananias, "Go! This man is my chosen instrument to proclaim my name to the Gentiles and their kings and to the people of Israel. I will show him how much he must suffer for my name."

[40] Then Ananias went to the house and entered it. Placing his hands on Saul, he said, "Brother Saul, the Lord—Jesus, who

appeared to you on the road as you were coming here—has sent me so that you may see again and be filled with the Holy Spirit." Immediately, something like scales fell from Saul's eyes, and he could see again. He got up and was baptized, and after taking some food, he regained his strength.

To call Ananias unwilling would be accurate. But he went to the house on Straight Street anyway.

I wonder how Ananias felt as he entered the house. Surely, he trusted Jesus, but at the same time, his heart had to be racing. You can tell that Jesus was with him, though. Ananias' healing through Jesus' power set Saul off on a journey of grace and suffering that I'll talk about further in the next chapter.

Leaving Yourself Exposed

Danger has been defined as "exposure or liability to injury, pain, harm, or loss."[41] I feel like that's a fair definition. Not all danger has to do with physical harm. Danger could also expose you financially, emotionally, with your reputation, etc.

When you leave safety for any kind of danger on behalf of Christ, as Ananias did, you are leaving your comfort zone and taking a risk. I would say that even kindness carries risk. You might have to give of your money or time. You might be late to your scheduled event. Your kindness could be rejected. You could experience physical danger. You leave yourself exposed, in small or large ways, when you're kind to another person.

German pilot Franz Stigler faced such a choice when considering kindness in 1943, during World War II. German fighter aircraft had severely damaged "Ye Olde Pub," an American B-17 Flying Fortress. Even the compass was damaged on the American craft, which meant the pilot was flying toward the enemy rather than away.

An ace with 27 victories, Stigler was given the order to track and shoot down the crippled plane. But as he got closer, he saw that the plane was very damaged. Stigler could also see how the pilot, Lt. Charlie Brown, was desperately trying to save the plane, its remaining crew, and his own life.

The easy choice for Stigler was to shoot down the plane and be done with the job. Instead, he decided to guide and escort the B-17 toward a safe zone unoccupied by the Germans.

After completing this task, Stigler saluted Brown and returned to his base. The German told his unit that he had shot down the B-17. [iii]

In one of those stories that sounds like Hollywood wrote it, Brown tracked down Stigler almost 50 years later to thank him. They became late-life friends, both dying five years later, just months apart. [42]

Stigler's act of mercy was as dangerous as it was courageous and humane. If discovered, he would have been exposed to severe consequences. Instead, the fighter pilot chose kindness instead of destruction.

Building with Faith, Confidence and Endurance

As I said before, exposure to danger can come in various ways. What about continually accepting a trust zone that combines physical danger, financial stress, and long-term damage to reputation?

When I visited Germany in 2023, I got a chance to not only visit Cologne Cathedral, a UNESCO World Heritage site, but to take a "behind-the-scenes" tour that showed me and taught me the cathedral's amazing history.

---

iii   The crew of "Ye Olde Pub." Lt. Charlie Brown, the pilot, is the leftmost man kneeling.

[43] In 1164, the Archbishop of Cologne, Rainald of Dassel, acquired the relics of the Three Kings which the Holy Roman Emperor, Frederick Barbarossa, had taken from the Basilica of Sant'Eustorgio, Milan, Italy. Church fathers felt these relics, believed to be the Magi that visited the infant Jesus, deserved a magnificent cathedral in which to house them. The cornerstone of the Gothic-style cathedral was laid in 1248.

The early architects and master builders envisioned the entire cathedral as it exists today. The vision for the cathedral was bold and unheard of. The twin spires would be the tallest in the world. The sanctuary was massive. A large, golden shrine of the Three Kings would be placed near the altar.

What strikes me most is that the vision was unachievable with the engineering, science, and technology of the 13th century. The master builders started forward in faith and confidence, believing that they would solve what they could, and future generations would figure out the rest.

Because the science for such a gigantic structure wasn't understood, the master builders proceeded by trial and error. The first seemingly insurmountable task was how to create support for such an enormous sanctuary. The master builders copied from the flying buttresses of a Gothic church in France, but the science was not well understood, and most efforts consisted of trial and error. At Cologne, the master builders eventually had to deploy outer buttresses to support the inner buttresses.

This process repeated itself for a couple of hundred years, gradually learning as they went. I don't have an account of how many lives were lost building the cathedral, but you would think that some were lost, and others were impaired from trial and error plus the sheer scope of the construction.

The cathedral continued being built until 1473, when the master builders encountered a showstopper. While assembling the first spire, they realized the technology was not in place to surpass a certain height. The spire work was stopped, while other cathedral construction continued for a century. Then all work ceased during the 16th century.

Shown in this engraving from 1820, the medieval crane used to lift the stones to the spire remained in place for nearly 400 years. Four hundred years!

[44] Seen first when approaching the city, the lonely crane became the symbol of Cologne. Generations came and went with no progress made on the cathedral. You can imagine the ridicule that the Cologne Cathedral leadership faced, unable to finish what they had started. An unfulfilled cathedral housed the Magi relics for centuries.

Finally, technology caught up with the vision. Cologne Cathedral construction resumed in 1842; the medieval crane ceremonially lifted the first stone, then was permanently retired (though it remained in place for more than a decade). By 1880, the vision was completed, and Cologne had built the tallest structure on earth at the time.

Cologne Cathedral's leadership had paid enormous sums, risked life and limb of its workers, and endured ridicule, but their faithfulness paid off. Not only was their faith evident in the overall structure, but in the details. I was impressed by the incredible detail of features 300 feet and higher – angels, gargoyles, intricate carvings – that would never be clearly seen from the ground. Yet the master builders and stonemasons knew God would see their work, and they planned and carved with great skill to honor the Lord.

This is what happens when you hear Jesus' call to "Go!" and respond to it.

You take whatever you have and whatever you are and allow it to be used on the Lord's behalf. Whenever I have done this, my experience is that God has blessed the effort and multiplied the results, a smaller version of Ananias' daring that was multiplied through the work of the Apostle Paul and the spread of the Christian church.

Summary of "Leaving Safety for Danger"

Big Thought:
Sometimes God's call carries greater risk and exposure, but also greater benefits to his kingdom.

Core Passage:
Acts 9: 10-19a

Key verse: But the Lord said to Ananias, "Go! This man is my chosen instrument to proclaim my name to the Gentiles and their kings and to the people of Israel. I will show him how much he must suffer for my name."

The Comfort Zone:
Protecting our physical health and what we have accumulated – money, possessions, reputations, and more.

The Trust Zone:
Permitting anything we have and are to be used for the Lord's service, trusting Jesus' promise to be with us.

Yielding Your Privilege for Humble Service

Saul had leveraged his long-time connection with the high priest to get what he wanted: Letters to synagogues in Damascus, authorizing him to persecute members of the Christian sect that had fled to that region.

Saul enjoyed a unique status emerging from his privilege. Born and raised in the Greek city of Tarsus, a center of education and philosophy, Saul's wealthy Jewish family had attained Roman citizenship. He was able to navigate across three cultures, using his Jewish name Saul (after the first king of Israel who came from Saul's tribe of Benjamin) in Jewish circles, and using his Latin name Paul when dealing with Romans and Greeks.

Highly educated in schooling, Saul was also highly educated in Pharisaic teachings. He studied under a leading Pharisee teacher, Gamaliel the elder, in Jerusalem.

These Christians bothered Saul for their heresies, such as disbelieving God's residence in the temple, their understanding of the Messiah, and even their proclamation of a hanged man as Savior when clearly, Deuteronomy had taught that "a hanged man is accursed by God." [45]

Then something happened that changed Saul's life, causing him to yield his privilege for humble service. Acts 9: 3-9 reads:

[46] As he neared Damascus on his journey, suddenly a light from heaven flashed around him. He fell to the ground and heard a voice say to him, "Saul, Saul, why do you persecute me?"

"Who are you, Lord?" Saul asked.

"I am Jesus, whom you are persecuting," he replied. "Now get up and go into the city, and you will be told what you must do."

The men traveling with Saul stood there speechless; they heard the sound but did not see anyone. Saul got up from the ground, but when he opened his eyes he could see nothing. So they led him by the hand into Damascus. For three days he was blind, and did not eat or drink anything.

As we've seen earlier, Ananias was tasked to heal Saul, who became the greatest missionary in Christian history, using the name Paul as he took the message of Jesus to the Gentile world.

Paul's Privilege

Think about the privileges that Paul gave up in order to modestly serve as an ambassador for Christ:

- <u>Wealth</u> – his family was wealthy enough to acquire Roman citizenship and to have him educated at an elite school in Jerusalem.
- <u>Education</u> – Both in Tarsus and Jerusalem, Paul became learned and was adept in multiple languages.
- <u>Location</u> – Tarsus was an ideal place for learning and exposure to multiple cultures.
- <u>Ethnic status</u> – The combination of Jewish heritage and Roman citizenship was rare.
- <u>Connections</u> – Between his Pharisaic schooling, his wealthy father's network, and his own connections through his tent-making skill, Paul had access to all sorts of people across three cultures.
- <u>Status</u> – Within the Jewish culture, Paul considered himself the brightest and the best, stating in Philippians 3: 4b-6:

> If someone else thinks they have reasons to put confidence in the flesh, I have more: circumcised on the eighth day, of the people of Israel, of the tribe of Benjamin, a Hebrew of Hebrews; in regard to the law, a Pharisee; as for zeal, persecuting the church; as for righteousness based on the law, faultless.

No question, Paul was a formidable man with everything going for him. Yet the Lord told Ananias, "I will show him how much he must suffer for my name."

And suffer Paul did: Through beatings, shipwrecks, imprisonment, sickness, "a thorn in his flesh," and more, Paul suffered for the gospel of Christ. He gave up his comfort zone of privilege for humble service, always seeing himself as the least apostle due to his prior persecution of Christians. He entered a trust zone with Jesus as his leader.

The Night and Day Life of a Saint

Another person who journeyed from privilege to humble service was Francesco di Pietro di Bernardone, whom we know as St. Francis of Assisi. He was born in the late 12th century into a wealthy family; his father was an Italian cloth merchant, while his mother was French (supposedly this is why he was named Francesco).[47]

His privileged upbringing gave him skills; Francis could speak Latin and French and was adept at archery, wrestling, and horsemanship. He was also spoiled, indulging himself with fine food, wine, and wild celebrations.[48] He was known as a leader among Assisi's young men.

Francis' life changed after he eagerly went off to the war between Assisi and Perugia in 1202. But he was captured and imprisoned for a year in a dank, underground cell, where he began to experience visions of God.

A signal of his transformation, after the war, was the legend of his encounter with a leper. Prior to the war, Francis would have run from the leper, but on this occasion, his behavior was very different. Viewing the leper as a symbol of moral conscience — or as Jesus incognito — Francis embraced and kissed him. After this incident, Francis felt an indescribable freedom. His earlier lifestyle had lost all of its appeal. [49]

Eventually Francis had a falling out with his father over his new, zealous Christian service. In a famous event, his father dragged him before the local bishop; Francis stripped off all his clothes, gave them and his money to his father, and declared that God was his only father.

Fortunately, the bishop hastily provided some basic clothes to him, and Francis went on his way.

⁵⁰ Living a life of poverty, repairing damaged churches, and preaching, Francis eventually convinced Pope Innocent III to approve the founding of his new order, the Franciscan Friars.

Probably no one in history has set out as seriously as did Francis to imitate the life of Christ and to carry out so literally Christ's work in Christ's own way. While committed to poverty, it was not mere external poverty he sought but the total denial of self. ⁵¹

It was only two years after Francis died in 1224 that he became venerated as a saint.

Like Paul, Francis yielded his privilege for humble service. His privileges mirrored many of Paul's: Wealth, education, dual preferred ethnicity, status.

What Does Privilege Look Like?

One of the problems of privilege is that one cannot see the forest for the trees; when you are within it, it's hard to realize what exists outside of it as well as what it looks like from the outside.

To Paul and Francis, wealth, a good education, favored ethnicity, social status, and connections were normal.

It wasn't until they recognized something greater in the Gospel that they fully recognized their advantages – and sought to give them up.

Paul was also able to channel his privilege into his mission. His education and worldliness allowed him to communicate with people in different regions according to how they understood things; for example, his astute recognition in Athens of the worship of an "unknown god" led him to identify that god as the God we know through Jesus Christ.. Paul's repurposed privilege allowed him to become a powerful missionary.

It takes humility and soul searching to identify your advantages and how you are viewed by others less fortunate than you are, to fully see and accept what their lives look like without such advantages, and to determine to do something about it.

If privilege is your comfort zone, it is important to view your privilege from the outside and recognize the advantages you possess. When you enter the trust zone of lowly Christian service, with the Holy Spirit's help you are able to lift others up through your own denial of privilege, leveraging remnants of it for a greater good.

Then you can fulfill the Bible's most urgent calls to help those on the underside of society, as in Zechariah 7: 9-10:

> "This is what the Lord Almighty says: 'Administer true justice; show mercy and compassion to one another. Do not oppress the widow or the fatherless, the foreigner or the poor. Do not plot evil against each other.'"

Perhaps none of us are worthy of the sainthood of Paul and Francis. But we can all carry out faithful lives worthy of a Jesus follower through introspection, self-denial, and action.

Summary of "Yielding Your Privilege for Humble Service"

Big Thought:
It's hard to see our own privilege. But when we do, we should give it up or leverage it well to diminish ourselves for the benefit of others.

Core Passage:
Acts 9: 3-9

Key verse: "Who are you, Lord?" Saul asked. "I am Jesus, whom you are persecuting," he replied. "Now get up and go into the city, and you will be told what you must do."

The Comfort Zone:
Using our privilege to serve our own needs.

The Trust Zone:
Yielding our privilege to serve Christ.

Journeying from Separation to Brotherhood

What a complex band the disciples were! I've already shown how a third of them were Zealots, originally interested more in the overthrow of Roman rule in the region than in the loving messaging of Jesus. What I want to show now is a problem that could have disrupted any harmony the disciples had, as an enemy of the Zealots was also a disciple.

[52] His name was Matthew, also known as Levi. Matthew was a tax collector when Jesus called him to discipleship. He's possibly the only disciple who got away with temporarily stalling Jesus' call to follow him. Matthew threw a party for Jesus before he hit the road with Jesus and the other disciples.

Here's how it happened, according to Luke 5: 27-32.

After this, Jesus went out and saw a tax collector by the name of Levi sitting at his tax booth. "Follow me," Jesus said to him, and Levi got up, left everything and followed him.

119

[53] Then Levi held a great banquet for Jesus at his house, and a large crowd of tax collectors and others were eating with them. But the Pharisees and the teachers of the law who belonged to their sect complained to his disciples, "Why do you eat and drink with tax collectors and sinners?"

Jesus answered them, "It is not the healthy who need a doctor, but the sick. I have not come to call the righteous, but sinners to repentance."

Tax collectors were considered sinners by the Pharisees and traitors by everyone else. Either directly or indirectly, tax collectors worked for the Romans, so they were seen as part of the occupier's ranks.

Not only that, but tax collectors tended to cheat people of their money, as they had wide latitude on how much to collect, what to collect (they might take your donkey), and why to collect. William Barclay comments:

If a man was traveling on a road, he might have to pay a tax for using the road, a tax on his cart, on its wheels, on its axle, and on the beast which drew the cart.[54]

No wonder tax collectors weren't popular! But they *were* rich. So, Matthew certainly had the money to fund a feast for Jesus. And no wonder the Zealots might have harbored some hard feelings toward Matthew. He represented Rome. He represented oppression. He represented everything against which they were fighting.

Most likely, Matthew also represented one more problem: A family rift.

Were They Brothers?

The Bible is not conclusive on this point, but there is evidence that Matthew and one of the Zealots, James the son of Alphaeus, were brothers.

Scripture tells us little about James the son of Alphaeus (who is also known as James the Younger or James the Lesser). From scripture, we know his name. We know he was a disciple.

[55] Also, we know that the mother of James the Younger, Mary, was present at the cross, one of the women grouped nearby to observe Jesus' crucifixion.

There are two small clues indicating that Matthew and James the son of Alphaeus were brothers. The first is the father's name, Alphaeus. Mark attributes the same paternal name to Matthew when Jesus calls him in Mark 2: 14:

As he walked along, he saw Levi son of Alphaeus sitting at the tax collector's booth. "Follow me," Jesus told him, and Levi got up and followed him.

Certainly there were many people who could have been named Alphaeus. But it's interesting that the reader has to connect these possible dots themselves. Scripture doesn't call out this brotherly connection, and it may well be a false one. But scholars seem to generally consider Matthew and James as being sons of the same Alphaeus.

The second clue is positioning within disciple lists. In all three Gospel lists of disciples, the Zealots are grouped together at the end. The first Zealot in each list is James the son of Alphaeus. In Mark and Luke, the last non-Zealot listed, preceding James the son of Alphaeus, is Thomas, who is preceded by Matthew.

But not so in the Gospel of Matthew, of which Matthew is historically considered to be the source if not the author. There's a subtle switch in our core passage, Matthew 10: 2-4.

> These are the names of the twelve apostles: first, Simon (who is called Peter) and his brother Andrew; James son of Zebedee, and his brother John; Philip and Bartholomew; Thomas and Matthew the tax collector; James son of Alphaeus, and Thaddaeus; Simon the Zealot and Judas Iscariot, who betrayed him.

Do you see the difference? The names of Matthew and Thomas are flipped, so that Matthew's name appears next to James, the son of Alphaeus. In other versions, they were separated; now they came close together.

Is there a reason for this? Perhaps the author wanted to position them closer together, similar to how James and John, sons of Zebedee, are listed next to each other.

It's also noteworthy that Matthew's is the only gospel that goes out of its way in the disciple list to remind everyone that Matthew was a tax collector. Once again, this highlights the schism within the disciple band between the tax collector and the Zealots.

Of course, I am largely speculating. Regardless of whether they were actually brothers by birth, there's no doubt that Matthew and James the Lesser were brothers under Christ as his disciples. Such brothers are expected to get along – aren't they?

Sorting through Squabbles

If you have siblings, you surely heard a parent say at some point, "Can't you kids get along?" We argue with our siblings at times. Sometimes our sibling relationships rip further apart.

I have three sisters, and we have had our share of squabbles and divisions. The disagreements stem from personalities, sibling order, family history, religious differences, political divisions, and more.

Yet we can usually function together if we focus on what unites us rather than on what divides us.

In recent years, we've gone through the final years and eventual passing of our mother. There has been a lot of postmortem activity regarding her possessions. We have largely been agreeable and held a united view of how to proceed.

Years ago, I started noticing an internal mental pattern that would occur in any personal or professional disagreement. I was holding onto my position with the thought, "It's the principle of the thing!" I felt like I had certain principles that I needed to stand by.

After awhile, I experienced a realization: It was **never** the principle of the thing. It was simple stubbornness. I kept telling myself a story where I was the sacred upholder of some valued principle, when in reality, I just didn't want to listen, didn't want to change my mind, didn't want to give in or be seen as weak.

That realization made a tremendous difference. It caused me to be more introspective about my motivations, determining whether it was my principle or my stubbornness I was defending. (Usually, it was the latter). It also caused me to listen more, to reflect more.

I'll admit, sometimes when I'm first challenged or presented with a new idea, I tend to reject it. But I'm pretty good at thinking it through later on and returning to the person to say, "I've thought about it, and you're right. I can get on board with your idea."

For decades, I worked in a highly technical field with a lot of smart people. I often described my job as "persuading really bright people that they are wrong, and sometimes learning in the process that they are actually right."

I learned humility in such arguments. This technical field was too complicated for any one person to know it all. Someone probably knew more than me sometimes. Still, I offered my own expertise and perspective in return. I improved at being able to logically state my case, understand their concerns, and reach a solution that we could all live with.

The ingredients for brotherhood and sisterhood and "human-hood," if I can make up a spanning word, are:

- Focus on what unites us rather than what divides us.
- Consider our own internal motivations that cause us to reject others' views.
- Listen and respond thoughtfully.
- Be humble. Be respectful about others' viewpoints while teaching others to respect yours.
- State your case persuasively to address their perspective and their concerns.
- Look for common ground and a workable solution.

Such actions overcome division and lead to unity.

Overcoming Christian Divisions

Even within Christian people, we can become divided – and reunited. A good example is the split that happened between Methodist founder John Wesley (along with his brother, hymn writer Charles) and his protégé, George Whitefield.

A rift developed when Whitefield, who claimed John Wesley as his spiritual father, began to investigate Calvinism and adopt its theology of predestination. Wesley despised predestination and wrote a sermon railing against it, and so the battle was on. Whitefield even set up his own church along the same street as Wesley's.

After a few years, the opponents realized that their quarrel of principles had gone too far. Both had moderated their views regarding the topic, while their parishioners had gone farther to extremes. One of Wesley's preachers described how Wesley and Whitefield had reached an "agreement to differ." Whitefield also gave up leading churches as he felt the call to become a "wayfaring witness," traveling between England, Scotland, and the American colonies.

While there were always sore feelings about the origins of division, there also became brotherhood. Both men took steps to ease the tensions between them and their factions. By the year of his death in 1770, Whitefield bequeathed each Wesley brother a mourning ring, "in token of my indissoluble union with them in heart and Christian affection, notwithstanding our difference in judgment about some particular points of doctrine."

At Whitefield's request, John Wesley preached the sermon at his funeral. [56]

Entering a Brotherly Trust Zone

I'm trying to imagine what it was like for Matthew and James the son of Alphaeus to create a brotherhood under Christ. Their unity would have come from Jesus himself; his cause and his principles would have governed them and brought about the Christian affection described by George Whitefield.

Still, I read in the Bible that the disciples would argue at times, act with pettiness, and not fully understand Jesus' cause and principles. There had to be rough moments of division. I'm imagining some impassioned mealtimes with the Zealots arguing against Roman rule while Matthew called for practicality in dealing with the occupiers.

At the end of the day, the disciples were united by Jesus and become his apostles, spreading his church, and taking his message to the world. Matthew and his estranged brother James became true brothers in Christ as they worked shoulder to shoulder together.

Their comfort zone had been their principles – "the principle of the thing."

Matthew lived his greedy principle, and James lived his rebellious principle. They let worldly doctrines overrun them, and they were actually happy with those results – until they met Jesus.

In giving up cherished axioms, their common trust zone was to accept a greater authority than themselves, acting in brotherhood until the gracious rule of Christ.

Summary of "Journeying from Separation to Brotherhood"

Big Thought:
We easily become divided because we focus on differences and don't focus on what unites us.

Core Passage:
Matthew 10: 2-4

Key verse: These are the names of the twelve apostles: first, Simon (who is called Peter) and his brother Andrew; James son of Zebedee, and his brother John; Philip and Bartholomew; Thomas and Matthew the tax collector; James son of Alphaeus, and Thaddaeus; Simon the Zealot and Judas Iscariot, who betrayed him.

The Comfort Zone:
Accepting division as a cost of upholding our personal principles.

The Trust Zone:
Bonding in brotherhood or sisterhood with individuals who hold different opinions as we cherish Christ's principles.

Implementing Jesus' Vision of Loving Unity

Do you remember this hymn?

> We are one in the Spirit, we are one in the Lord;
> And we pray that all unity will one day be restored.
> And they'll know we are Christians by our love. [57]

In a way, it's sad that the lyrics to this famous hymn had to be written to remind us Christians to be unified by love. But it's a necessary reminder. Too often when we look across Christianity, the divisions come to mind first instead of the shared love.

Perhaps it's always been this way. Perhaps it's human nature to divide rather than to unite.

[58] Jesus knew this. That's why in some of the final words of his lengthy prayer at the Last Supper, Christ looked forward into the future to pray for the unity of future believers (John 17: 20-23):

"My prayer is not for *(my current disciples)* alone. I pray also for those who will believe in me through their message, that all of them may be one, Father, just as you are in me and I am in you. May they also be in us so that the world may believe that you have sent me. I have given them the glory that you gave me, that they may be one as we are one— I in them and you in me—so that they may be brought to complete unity. Then the world will know that you sent me and have loved them even as you have loved me."

Jesus was a prophet, among other things, and he knew that unity would be difficult. It's more comfortable for us to form and defend our opinions than it is to bend to someone else. Jesus says that the standard for unity is the unity between the Father and the Son. That's the trust zone he wants us to enter.

Jesus Speaks to Future Disciples

Reflecting on the passage above, the NIV Study Bible points out:

Jesus' prayer is a rebuke of the groundless and often bitter divisions among believers…Believers are to be characterized by humility and service, just as Christ was, and it is on them that God's glory rests. [59]

I would hope that we are characterized by humility and service. I'm not sure the latest opinion polls would describe followers of Christ in this way.

Remember that Christ's desire for unity has a purpose: To let the world "know that you sent me and have loved them even as you have loved me." In other words, Jesus is saying that the spread of the gospel relies on the loving unity of his followers through the generations and centuries.

Reflecting on this point, David Platt writes:

> Wow. To think that the world realizing that Jesus has been sent by the father to be the savior of the world, that our unity as followers of Jesus has a direct effect on that realization being a reality in the world.
>
> If we are not unified, we hinder testimony to Jesus. We hinder the spread of the gospel with a lack of unity. And let's be clear, this is not some low-level, manufactured, manipulated, artificial, superficial unity. Like, let's just all get along. Regardless of what we believe, let's all be unified regardless of how we live.
>
> That's not the picture. This is a unity that is grounded in Jesus. This is a unity that is grounded in the truth of Jesus. The words of Jesus, the person of Jesus, the spirit of Jesus, the commands of Jesus. This is where our unity is grounded, and Jesus prays that we might experience it so that the world might know his love…
>
> Our unity is not in our politics, it's not in our ethnicity, it's not in our preferences. It's not in our socioeconomic status. *(Jesus has)* made it possible for us to be unified in a way that transcends all of these things. [60]

How do we achieve this unity? That's the hard part, isn't it?

Ruined by Our Selfishness

I've always been struck by the lyrics of the upbeat song, "We Can Work It Out" by the Beatles. On the surface, it seems to make an appeal for compromise – "we can work it out." But if you read the lyrics with a discerning eye, it's not talking about compromise at all.

Here are the two verses and chorus:

> Try to see it my way,
> Do I have to keep on talking till I can't go on?
> While you see it your way,
> Run the risk of knowing that our love may soon be gone.
> We can work it out,
> We can work it out.
> Think of what you're saying.
> You can get it wrong and still you think that it's alright.
> Think of what I'm saying,
> We can work it out and get it straight, or say good night.
> We can work it out,
> We can work it out. [61]

The person speaking in the song isn't interested in compromise; they're interested in winning! There are digs about "seeing it your way" and "you can get it wrong and still you think that it's alright."

Oh, it's all done in the name of harmony, on the surface. But there's also a threat: If you don't agree with me, "our love may soon be gone". You need to "get it straight, or say good night."

Clearly, the problem is the attitude that "I'm right, and you're wrong." This attitude permeates so much of society and so much of Christianity today. Christians experience friction between denominations and within denominations, making both outsiders and insiders wonder, "What's going on?"

I like to joke that the world would be great if everyone did everything <u>my</u> way. But deep down, isn't that what most of us believe? If everyone just saw things as I do and did them that way, then everything would be fine.

In his book, <u>Running While Black</u>, Rick Hightower talks about the concept of lived experiences:

We are a collection of our lived experiences. These lived experiences help shape us. And because we experience the world with our whole selves, our observations are valid. [62]

When we diminish others' viewpoints, we diminish their lived experiences. We diminish their very lives. In the worst case, this is called gaslighting - a form of psychological abuse in which a person or group causes someone to question their own sanity, memories, or perception of reality. [63] At best, it means we don't show respect for others' opinions.

Our unity is ruined by our selfishness. I've long said that the root of all sin is selfishness. As an example, consider the seven deadly sins; each one contains a dimension of selfishness:

- Pride
- Greed
- Wrath
- Envy
- Lust
- Gluttony
- Sloth

So let's do the math:

If disunity = selfishness
and selfishness = the root of all sin
then disunity = sin. Pure and simple.

What Do We Do?

OK, Cecil, disunity is bad, and unity is good. Now what?
Uh, that's the hard part.
It's the hard part because human history has shown that we

become fragmented, whether on a person-to-person level or on a national or international level.

It's the hard part because, despite what I've written so far, most of you reading this still believe that disunity is someone else's problem. If only <u>they</u> would change their views, then we can work it out.

I have two keywords for you to consider: Humility and Glory.

The Humility of Christ

When the Apostle Paul sensed disunity in the church at Philippi, he wrote a letter to them, saying this in Philippians 2, verses 1-5 and 8:

> Therefore if you have any encouragement from being united with Christ, if any comfort from his love, if any common sharing in the Spirit, if any tenderness and compassion, then make my joy complete by being like-minded, having the same love, being one in spirit and of one mind. Do nothing out of selfish ambition or vain conceit. Rather, in humility value others above yourselves, not looking to your own interests but each of you to the interests of the others.

In your relationships with one another, have the same mindset as Christ Jesus:

... And being found in appearance as a man, he humbled himself by becoming obedient to death — even death on a cross!

134

What are the keywords and key phrases in this passage?

- Like-minded
- Same love
- One in spirit and of one mind
- Humility
- Value others above yourself
- Look to the interests of others

Despite possessing all power, as we see in Jesus' miracles for example, Christ prefers to humbly display his weakness. He started with a lowly birth in place and in status. He proclaimed in Matthew 11 how he is "gentle and humble in heart." He allowed himself to be tortured and killed physically so that all might be saved spiritually.

The result of humility is to possess the same minds, the same spirit, the same love.

The Glory of God

A negative set of keywords in the Philippians passage included selfish ambition and vain conceit.

This is the negative side of human nature. The people of Israel were not satisfied with God as their king and insisted on a king of their own. But their earthly kings either drove them to ruin or joined them on the path to ruin. The people wanted their own glory, like every other nation had glory, so they lost and recovered the glory of God in an endless cycle.

Again, what did Jesus pray earlier that he wanted for us future believers? From John 17: 22:

> I have given them the glory that you gave me, that they may be one as we are one— I in them and you in me—so that they may be brought to complete unity.

Do we refuse God's glory through our selfish ambition and vain conceit? Indeed we do. Because we refuse God's glory, we refuse the complete unity that Christ offers and desires.

Like the Israelites, we can only experience God's glory by accepting God as ruler of our lives. When we experience disunity, either in personal relationships or in corporate deliberations, it's because we are grabbing the throne from God once again.

We have a spiritual problem that manifests itself in many ways.

Our comfort zone involves our selfishness and our vanity. We refuse God's leadership to make our own path. We do the opposite of what Paul says in Philippians, valuing ourselves more than others, and acting out of selfish ambition and vain conceit.

Our trust zone is when we swallow hard and humbly, accepting Jesus' will for us to be unified, humbly listening and interacting with others, and thus finding the glory of God once again illuminates our lives.

When this happens, we can implement Jesus' vision of loving unity. It's not the formula we would expect. But it's the formula the Bible gives us.

Summary of "Implementing Jesus' Vision of Loving Unity."

Big Thought:
Jesus envisions and wills for his followers to be united in order to live with God's glory within us and to effectively spread the gospel.

Core Passage:
John 17: 20-23

Key verse: I have given them the glory that you gave me, that they may be one as we are one— I in them and you in me—so that they may be brought to complete unity.

Key verse from Philippians 2: 1-5, 8: Do nothing out of selfish ambition or vain conceit. Rather, in humility value others above yourselves, not looking to your own interests but each of you to the interests of the others.

The Comfort Zone:
Holding ourselves as better than others, through selfish ambition or vain conceit.

The Trust Zone:
Believing that emulating Jesus' humility will foster unity among believers and shine the light of God's glory within us.

Summary of Comfort and Trust Zones

Chapter	The Comfort Zone	The Trust Zone
Taking Risks	Self-interest and self-preservation.	Self-denial to serve the Lord's interests.
Going All-In	Accepting Jesus on our terms.	Following Jesus on his terms.
Replacing Status-Seeking with Servanthood	Chasing and using worldly acclaim to feel better about ourselves.	Humbly serving others so that others will feel better about Jesus.
Releasing Our Sins and Our Stones	Being so comfortable with our own sin that we are comfortable in judging others.	Trusting Jesus to do his job of judgment and grace, and following his will to do our job of dispensing mercy.
Looking at Jesus Rather Than Obstacles	Focusing on overcoming obstacles so we can return to normal as quickly as possible.	Keeping our eyes on Jesus and relying on him to be a very present help in times of trouble.
Exchanging the Familiar for a New Calling	A trust zone that has become a comfort zone over time.	A new challenge to shake you out of your comfort zone and deepen your commitment to Christ.

Chapter	The Comfort Zone	The Trust Zone
Relinquishing Certainty, Embracing Uncertainty	Our quest for certainty through earthly means in a scary, uncertain world.	Embracing ambiguity and uncertainty in your life while leaning on Jesus for your certainty.
Trading Governments and Empires for Jesus' Kingdom	Reliance on governments, political parties, and political leaders to save us.	Opening our hearts and pursuing others' hearts to serve Jesus' aim to live in those hearts.
Leaving Safety for Danger	Protecting our physical health and what we have accumulated – money, possessions, reputations, and more.	Permitting anything we have and are to be used for the Lord's service, trusting Jesus' promise to be with us.
Yielding Your Privilege for Humble Service	Using our privilege to serve our own needs.	Yielding our privilege to serve Christ.
Journeying from Separation to Brotherhood	Accepting division as a cost of upholding our personal principles.	Bonding in brotherhood or sisterhood with individuals who hold different opinions as we cherish Christ's principles.
Implementing Jesus' Vision of Loving Unity	Holding ourselves as better than others, through selfish ambition or vain conceit.	Believing that emulating Jesus' humility will foster unity among believers and shine the light of God's glory within us.

Go Deeper with the Participant's Guide

Every book and video study from Cecil Taylor Ministries includes the opportunity to go deeper in your study with the purchase of an accompanying Participant's Guide.

For each chapter, the Participant's Guide offers a week-long study of the topic, with exercises, activities, meditations, and / or further Bible study. It will enrich you individually and as a group if you study together.

The Participant's Guide is available in online bookstores and at CecilTaylorMinistries.com. Please visit **https://Store.CecilTaylorMinistries.com** to find it, or access the store via the QR Code below.

Please Review This Book!

Reviews are the lifeblood of an author. For the average author, like me, books simply can't be found and shared without people like you reviewing them.

Reviews, of course, help my book sales. But reviews also help fellow readers. They also help spread the message generally; if you find this to be a book others should read, you are spreading goodness by writing a review.

Please review this book! Regardless of where you purchased it, I would appreciate you visiting popular online book web site(s) and leaving a review. You do not have to have purchased the book on that site, typically, to leave a review, although I understand that a famous one requires a small purchase amount over the past year if you didn't buy the book there. Even negative reviews are helpful, believe it or not, so say whatever you must.

People tell me they don't know how to leave a review. This process will vary slightly by book site, but generally speaking, here is the process:

1. Navigate to the book's page on the bookseller web site.
2. Scroll down until you see the rating and reviews for the book. (Look for stars!)
3. Nearby, there will be a link to be able to leave a review yourself. Click on that link.
4. Typically you'll be asked to give a star rating, to create a review title, and to write a review. The review does not have to be long; only two or three sentences are fine. But

write all that you want beyond that, as longer reviews are
helpful to create a picture for other readers.

5.   Submit the review.

Thank you for your reviews. Thank you for sharing this book
with others, either verbally or by handing them your copy. Thank
you for posting about it on social media. Your effort will help
someone else if you do.

Free Mini-Book Offer: The Disciple Profiles

To me, it's intriguing to learn more about Jesus' disciples, as you've done in this book. Would you like to learn even more?

I've written a free mini-book about the disciples. Using scripture, historical accounts, research books, and legends, I've put together a profile of each disciple. You'll find out more about their backgrounds, their words and actions, and what happened to them after Christ's resurrection.

To receive your e-copy of the mini-book, you only need to register at **https://www.ceciltaylorministries.com/free-gift-of-disciple-profiles. This is an INSIDER page on my web site only accessible from here!** You can also visit the page using the QR code below.

Free Mini-Book Offer: The Eternal Trust Zone

The ultimate Jesus trust zone is eternal life. We enter that trust zone through belief in our Savior.

Yet, eternal life is still a mystery. What did Jesus say about it? I've captured the scripture and accompanying explanations in this insightful mini-book that will help you achieve eternal life with him.

To receive your e-copy of the mini-book, you only need to register at **https://www.ceciltaylorministries.com/free-gift-of-trust-zone-eternal. This is an INSIDER page on my web site only accessible from here!** You can also visit the page using the QR code below.

About the Author

I was born into the family of a preacher and a teacher (eventually, after she raised four children). Those are the roots that have formed Cecil Taylor Ministries.

But those aren't the only roots. I feel like everything in my diverse life has led to this moment and to this ministry:

- My varied career in high tech software development and product management, in sports broadcasting, and in running my own side businesses.
- 30+ years in youth ministry, an adulthood of teaching adult Sunday School, 15 years of teaching parenting classes.
- Growing up in tiny rural towns, only venturing out of state once in my first 23 years, but eventually traveling to 24 countries on four continents.
- Being married 38 years and raising three children, one of which was adopted.
- Working overtime many times but also experiencing unemployment or underemployment for nearly six years out of a 10-year stretch.

In other words, a little bit of almost everything. All of those experiences inform my perspective in Cecil Taylor Ministries.

I'm going to tell you more about what I do in Cecil Taylor Ministries, but first let me tell you about who I am.

Someone once described me as a blend of serious and silly, which is an ideal mix for working with youth, by the way! I like to smile and laugh. Someone took a picture of me laughing in college, and my face was stretched out in a weird way. I commented on how strange I looked, but the person said, "But that's how you look!" I could live with that. I love to laugh.

I like to gently prank or fool people; I'm only searching for that singular moment of confusion that says, "Is this happening for real?" Then I let them in on what's happening.

I can be competitive, intense, driven, and fully Type A. I'm an extrovert who knows how to live with introverts. I don't know my scores for popular personality tests. I'm a natural leader and will fill a leadership void if one appears. I draw energy from people.

I've said (and have pretty much proven) that I can have a conversation with any stranger for five minutes. I genuinely like people, as frustrating as they can be. I will work the room at parties; actually, I've worked the room at funerals! I was recently at a wedding reception and told my wife Sara, "It drives me crazy to be in this room," and she knew why – I wanted to know everyone in the room, and it wasn't possible.

I am sure that I would love to talk to you someday.

As I pivot to Cecil Taylor Ministries, I must first point to God's call for me to be in this ministry. God is the CEO; I'm the COO. My external slogan is "Teaching Christians to live a 7-day practical faith," but my internal slogan is derived from 2 Chronicles 20: 12, "I do not know what to do, but my eyes are on you."

About the Author

The reason my ministry is focused on teaching Christians how to live a 7-day practical faith is that people would tell me after Sunday School classes, "I can do this Christian stuff on Sundays, but it's hard to do it the rest of the week." My goal is to help people live a daily faith, from Sunday to Sunday, not only because it honors God, but because it helps fulfill Jesus' goal that "I came that they may have life, and have it abundantly."

This is my third book, following two books that were both fortunate enough to win awards at Christian writers' conferences.

- *The Next Thing: A Christian Model for Dealing with Crisis in Personal Life* explores a four-part model for addressing any crisis, using the central idea of facing the next thing in front of you. The work is deeply personal.
- *Live Like You're Loved* underscores the four Biblical truths that you are loved by God, forgiven by God, sent by God into the world, and an eternal creature invited to eternal relationship with God. Then I outline 16 memorable steps, called SAIL steps, that help translate that knowledge into a new lifestyle in which you live like you're loved, forgiven, sent, and eternal.

I have another book coming out in parallel to this one: *Unison Parenting*. It leverages my experiences as a parent and as a teacher of parents to help parents in a wide array of situations to speak in unison to the child and avoid the pitfalls that lead to family conflicts.

I could spend much more ink on my ministry's other video series, blogs, podcasts, video devotionals, speaking engagements, and so on. But instead, for current information on the Instant Content products and services available through Cecil Taylor Ministries, please visit **CecilTaylorMinistries.com**.

I pray that this book blesses your life and draws you closer to God. And I hope that I'm blessed to someday learn that it made a difference.

Cecil's Social Media URLs and QR Codes

Cecil Taylor Ministries Home Page
https://www.CecilTaylorMinistries.com

Cecil Taylor Ministries Facebook Page
https://www.facebook.com/ceciltaylorministries

Cecil Taylor Ministries YouTube Channel
https://www.youtube.com/channel/UCHP_khu3r77ubl5jvHsf5-w

Cecil Taylor's LinkedIn Page
https://www.linkedin.com/in/ceciltaylor/

Free Offer: Subscription to Cecil Taylor Ministries Plus Gift

I invite you to become a subscriber to Cecil Taylor Ministries. There is no charge. You will receive a monthly newsletter from me, as well as a few introductory emails in the beginning. The newsletter keeps you in touch with me and the ministry, as well as sharing advice on various faith and church topics, and a devotional.

When you subscribe online, you will receive a free gift from me. The gift may vary over time, depending on when you read this and subscribe; the first gift was a 30-day devotional guide.

By the way, if you register for any other free offer noted in this book, you will automatically be registered as a free subscriber as well.

Use the link and QR code for CecilTaylorMinistries.com shown in the Social Media / QR codes section. Either register via a pop-up box or by scrolling down to the orange box on the home page.

Gratitude

I am grateful for the encouragers who helped me get to this point, either through their support of this book's development and/or through their support of Cecil Taylor Ministries. Specifically:

- My core team of Sara Taylor and Connor Walden for editing and artwork, respectively, in addition to their encouragement for the project.
- My official reviewers, Jennifer Chamberlain and Lyvita Brooks, for their time and their endorsement of this project.
- The ANEW class at St. Andrew Methodist Church in Plano, Texas, for being a sounding board as I trialed the content.
- The Cecil Taylor Ministries Prayer Team that walks with me each week through prayer, encouragement, and spiritual sustenance.
- Finally, I am grateful to you for buying this book. I welcome your emailed feedback at Cecil@CecilTaylorMinistries.com, and I hope that you will accept one of the free offers so I can be in communication with you.

Endnotes

1   Photographic reproduction of "The Calling of Saint John and Saint Andrew" by James Tissot. This work is in the public domain in the United States and other countries/areas where the copyright term is the author's life plus 100 years or fewer.

2   https://www.restorativefaith.org/post/departure-why-i-left-the-church

3   Photographic reproduction of "The Parable of the Talents or Minas" by Willem de Poorter. This work is in the public domain in the United States and other countries/areas where the copyright term is the author's life plus 100 years or fewer.

4   Barclay, William. "The Gospel of Matthew Volume 2" (Revised Edition). Philadelphia: Westminster Press, 1975.

5   https://www.raystedman.org/thematic-studies/parables/to-risk-or-not-to-risk

6   https://www.raystedman.org/thematic-studies/parables/to-risk-or-not-to-risk

7   Photographic reproduction of *Feeding the Multitude* by an unknown 6th century artist. This work is in the public domain in the United States as it is in the public domain in its country of origin and other countries and areas where the copyright term is the author's life plus 100 years or fewer.

8   https://www.bibleref.com/John/6/John-6-61.html

9   Peale, Norman Vincent. *The Power of Positive Thinking," reprint edition.* Chicago: Touchstone, 2003.

10   Da Vinci, Leonardo. *The Last* Supper. This work is in the public domain in the United States because it was published (or registered with the U.S. Copyright Office) before January 1, 1928.

11   Edelfelt, Albert. *Jesus Washing the Feet of His Disciples.* This work is in the public domain in the United States as it is in the public domain in its country of origin and other countries and areas where the copyright term is the author's life plus 100 years or fewer.

12   Barclay, William. *The Gospel of John, Volume 2 (Revised Edition).* Philadelphia: Westminster Press, 1975.

13   Jones, E. Stanley. *The Christ of the Indian Road.* New York: Abingdon Press, 1925.

14   https://www.nbcnews.com/nightly-news/video/ alabama-farmer-secretly-paid-pharmacy-bills-for-those-in-need-162644549964

15   https://www.wvtm13.com/article/geraldine-alabama-man-secretly-donates-100-a-month-to-pharmacy-so-others-could-afford-their-medicine/42447381

16   Brueghell II, Pieter. *Christ and the Woman Taken in Adultery.* This work is considered public domain in the United States as it is in the public domain in its country of origin and other countries and areas where the copyright term is the author's life plus 100 years or fewer.

17   Barclay, William. *The Parables of Jesus.* Louisville: Westminster John Knox Press, 1999 (reprint).

18   Hall, Kay. *Beyond the Hidden Veil of Shame: One Woman's Postabortion Journey to a Settled and Peaceful Heart.* Bloomington, IN: Westbow Press, 2020.

19   The Barna Research Group and The Fermi Project, "A New Generation Expresses its Skepticism and Frustration with Christianity," September 2007.

20   https://www.psychologytoday.com/us/blog/living-eating-disorders/202110/why-do-we-judge-other-people

21   https://arcadiancounseling.com/why-we-judge-others-how-to-stop

22   Lashelle Lowe-Chardé, https://www.wiseheartpdx.org/posts/2022/1/27-understanding-judgment-and-criticism

23   Daniel of Uranc. *Jesus Walking on Water*. This work is considered public domain in the United States as it is in the public domain in its country of origin and other countries and areas where the copyright term is the author's life plus 100 years or fewer.

24   Jarnefelt, Eero. This work is considered public domain in the United States as it is in the public domain in its country of origin and other countries and areas where the copyright term is the author's life plus 100 years or fewer.

25   Raphael. *Christ's Charge to Peter*. This work is in the public domain in the United States as it is in the public domain in its country of origin and other countries and areas where the copyright term is the author's life plus 100 years or fewer.

26   A print from the Phillip Medhurst Collection of Bible illustrations in the possession of Revd. Philip De Vere at St. George's Court, Kidderminster, England. Licensed for all uses under Creative Commons Attribution-Share Alike 3.0 Unported license found at https://creativecommons.org/licenses/by-sa/3.0/deed.en.

27   Copping, Harold. *The Rich Young Ruler*. This work is considered public domain in the United States as it is in the public domain in its country of origin and other countries and areas where the copyright term is the author's life plus 100 years or fewer.

28   https://www.nytimes.com/2013/09/08/sports/football/the-cowboys-jones-has-the-midas-touch.html

29   Rabins, John. *Defined by Fire: Seven Life-Changing Lessons from Devastating Tragedy.* Firewall Press, 2020.

30   Barclay, William. "*The Master's Men.*" New York/Nashville: Abingdon Press, 1959.

31   Josephus. "The Antiquities of the Jews", 18, 1, 6.

32   Kalas, J. Ellsworth. "The Thirteen Apostles." Nashville: Abingdon Press, 1923 (copyright renewed 2022).

33   Backer, Jacob Adriaensz. "The Tribute Money." Public domain in the United States as the copyright expired at the artist's death (1651) plus 100 years in its country of origin.

34   Silver Denarius of Tiberius, Lugdunum (MANTIS). jpg. This file is made available under the Creative Commons CC0 1.0 Universal Public Domain Dedication.

35   https://www.newsweek.com/evangelicals-rejecting-jesus-teachings-liberal-talking-points-pastor-1818706

36   https://peggynoonan.com/302/

37   https://peggynoonan.com/302/

38   Unknown artist. *Thaddeus of Edessa.* This is in the public domain in the United States because this work is in the public domain in its country of origin and other countries and areas where the copyright term is the author's life plus 100 years or fewer.

39   van Dyck, Anthony. *Apostle Judas Thaddeus.* This is in the public domain in the United States because this work is in the public domain in its country of origin and other countries and areas where the copyright term is the author's life plus 100 years or fewer.

40   Ferri, Ciro. *Ananias of Damascus lays his hand on*

Saul. 17th century. This is in the public domain in the United States because this work is in the public domain in its country of origin and other countries and areas where the copyright term is the author's life plus 100 years or fewer.

41   https://merriam-webster.com/dictionary/danger

42   https://mindsetopia.com/inspiring-stories-of-mercy

43   Dronepicr, *Cologne Cathedral Aerial.* Licensed for use under Creative Commons Attribution Generic 2.0, described at https://creativecommons.org/licenses/by/2.0/deed.en

44   Winkles, Henry. Engraving of Cologne Cathedral from 1820. This work is in the public domain of the United States because it is in the public domain in its country of origin and other countries and areas where the copyright term is the author's life plus 100 years or fewer.

45   *Who's Who in the Bible.* Pleasantville, NY: Reader's Digest Association, 1994.

46   Speckaert, Hans. *Conversion of St. Paul on the Road to Damascus.* This work is in the public domain of the United States because it is in the public domain in its country of origin and other countries and areas where the copyright term is the author's life plus 100 years or fewer.

47   https://www.britannica.com/biography/Saint-Francis-of-Assisi

48   https://www.biography.com/religious-figures/saint-francis-of-assisi

49   https://www.biography.com/religious-figures/saint-francis-of-assisi

50   Fruytiers, Philip. *St. Francis of Assisi.* This work is in the public domain of the United States because it is in the public domain in its country of origin and other countries and areas where the copyright term is the author's life plus

100 years or fewer.

51   https://www.britannica.com/biography/Saint-Francis-of-Assisi/The-Franciscan-rule

52   van Dyke, Andrew. "Apostle Matthew" (Althorp). This work is in the public domain in its country of origin and other countries and areas where the copyright term is the author's life plus 100 years or fewer.

53   van Matteus, Roeping. *Calling of Matthew.* This file is made available under the Creative Commons CC0 1.0 Universal Public Domain Dedication.

54   Barclay, William. "The Master's Men." New York/Nashville: Abingdon Press, 1959.

55   Unknown artist. "Apostle James, son of Alphaeus". This work is in the public domain in its country of origin and other countries and areas where the copyright term is the author's life plus 100 years or fewer.

56   Walsh, J.D., https://christianhistoryinstitute.org/magazine/article/wesley-vs-whitefield

57   Scholtes, Peter. *"They'll Know We are Christians by Our Love."* Lyrics copyrighted 1966 F.E.L. Publications. Assigned 1991 Lorenz Publishing Company (Admin. by Lorenz Corporation).

58   Light, Chris. Authorized under Creative Commons Attribution-ShareAlike 4.0 International at https://creativecommons.org/licenses/by-sa/4.0/deed.en.

59   *The NIV Study Bible, 10th Anniversary Edition.* Copyright 1995 by The Zondervan Corporation, Grand Rapids, MI.

60   Platt, David. https://radical.net/podcasts/pray-the-word/jesus-praying-for-us-john-1720-21

61   https://genius.com/The-beatles-we-can-work-it-

out-lyrics. John Lennon / Paul McCarthey. © BMG Rights Management, Kobalt Music Publishing Ltd., Songtrust Ave, Sony/ATV Music Publishing LLC, Warner Chappell Music, Inc

62   Hightower, Rick. *Running While Black: Reflections of the Race of My Life*. Coppell, Texas: 2023.

63   https://www.medicalnewstoday.com/articles/ gaslighting

www.ingramcontent.com/pod-product-compliance
Lightning Source LLC
Chambersburg PA
CBHW071403120626
46546CB00002B/790